DRINKING DIARIES

WOMEN SERVE THEIR STORIES STRAIGHT UP

EDITED BY LEAH ODZE EPSTEIN **&** CAREN OSTEN GERSZBERG

SEAL PRESS

DRINKING DIARIES
Women Serve Their Stories Straight Up

Published by
Seal Press
A Member of the Perseus Books Group
1700 Fourth Street
Berkeley, California

Library of Congress Cataloging-in-Publication Data

Odze Epstein, Leah, 1966-
Drinking diaries : women serve their stories straight up / Leah Odze
Epstein and Caren Osten Gerszberg. -- 1st ed.
p. cm.
ISBN 978-1-58005-411-9
1. Women--Alcohol use. I. Osten Gerszberg, Caren, 1964- II. Title.
HV5137.O394 2012
362.292092'52--dc23
2012010256 (p. 57 – Part 2)

10 9 8 7 6 5 4 3 2

Cover design by Elke Barter
Interior design by Tabitha Lahr
Printed in the United States of America
Distributed by Publishers Group West

To our mothers

CONTENTS

PART 1 GIRLHOOD
CANDY IS DANDY, BUT LIQUOR IS QUICKER

PART 2 RELATIONSHIPS
HERE'S TO US!

PART 3 CULTURE
FROM BAILEYS TO MANISCHEWITZ

PART 4 FAMILY
DRINKING THE KOOL-AID

PART 5 REVELATIONS

TOO MUCH IS BARELY ENOUGH

INTRODUCTION

ASK ANY WOMAN YOU KNOW to scratch the surface, and she will find a drinking story. Whether we are drinking it or not, alcohol remains a potent part of our lives, like food and the Internet. The world is saturated with it, steeped in it. We confront alcohol everywhere we go—from home to the office party, date night to ladies' night, happy hour to sports sidelines. Even where alcohol is not present on the surface, it often lies beneath, a palpable absence.

We drink for different reasons: to quench thirst, to loosen up, because it tastes good, to enhance a meal, because we're addicted, to self medicate, as part of a ceremony, to celebrate, to mourn. We drink when we're happy. We drink when we're sad. And then there are the nondrinkers, for whom abstaining may be as much of an issue as drinking.

Whether our drinking is a choice or a compulsion, people rarely talk about its quotidian existence. It's easy to make the snide celebrity putdown or joke, or to label excessive drinking as a pathology. Extreme examples of abuse—from Amy Winehouse and Lindsay Lohan to Whitney Houston and Diane Schuler—are widely reported. And the resulting trickle-down deepens the culture of blame and shame around the subject of women and *all* drinking, as evidenced by the rise and fall of the Cocktail Mom. No wonder women keep their stories to themselves. (According to *Newsweek* magazine, 60 percent of American women drink.)

Our ultimate goal, from the Drinking Diaries blog to this book, has been to take women's stories out of the closet. There are plenty of memoirs by recovering alcoholics and countless books covering an array of women's issues—from love and marriage to family and career—but none addresses the spectrum of stories about women and drinking. How does a woman's experience with alcohol, both good and bad, affect her relationship with herself, her partner, her children, her friends, her community? How has drinking—our own and others'—really touched our lives?

The stories are typically hard to come by and rarely surface in small talk. But here you will read the details, the deep questions, the wide and wild range of drinking experiences. A dispatch from the real world of women and alcohol, the essays in this book tell of women who vary in age, experience, perspective, and culture. They tap into all aspects of drinking—the shameful, the escapist, the liberating, the celebratory, the sexual, and so on.

The idea for this book about women and drinking evolved from a night of . . . drinking. The two of us are friends and neighbors who enjoy sharing a bottle of wine over dinner with our families. Here's how it all began.

Leah

For my first-grade school photo, my alcoholic mother put my sailor dress on me inside out. She stopped drinking when I was nine years old. By the time I hit fourteen, my older sister was in rehab. I spent half my adolescence at self-help meetings, and although I would rather have been hanging out with my friends, I found the personal narratives of fall and redemption riveting. From high school to college student, writer to stay-at-home mom, I have run the gamut from abstainer to binge drinker.

Caren

I never used to give a second thought to keeping a bottle of wine in my fridge, chilling next to the milk, just as my mother did. My European parents drank every night with dinner, and my mother—a French, hidden-child survivor of the Holocaust—often bragged about how she'd

corrupted her American friends with the joys of a late afternoon glass
of wine. But later in life, my mother's wartime demons came back to
haunt her, and her social drinking morphed into need. Since then I—a
lover of wine in moderation—have been wrestling with what drinking
means to me.

CONVERSATIONS ABOUT OUR mothers evolved into discussions about our own drinking—the ups, the downs, the in-betweens. And then we wondered: Were there other women who also wanted to talk about drinking?

Together we sought to create an open forum for women who'd be interested in sharing their stories—without asking anyone to descend into a fluorescent-lit church basement. Since starting the Drinking Diaries blog in 2009, we've had more than a quarter million readers of all ages and from all over the world.

What we've uncovered is a wide spectrum of drinkers and attitudes about drinking that runs contrary to the rigid lines often drawn between problem drinkers and the rest of us. It turns out that the "rest of us" are a nuanced group—nondrinkers; occasional drinkers; passionate drinkers; daughters and mothers of drinkers, nondrinkers, and about-to-be drinkers; teen drinkers; middle-aged drinkers; Asian, Jewish, Italian, African American, and Muslim drinkers. The variations are endless.

The twenty-eight stories we've collected here—written by both prominent and new writers—are a testament to diversity, with themes spanning from celebration to revelation. In all the essays, drinking has left its mark.

The book begins with a section called "Girlhood," in which writers explore the effect that drinking—their own or others'—had on their younger selves. Childhood and adolescence are a time to observe the grown-ups drinking or to experiment with alcohol on one's own. In some cases, the imprint alcohol leaves during the early years carries through into adulthood with a vengeance; in others, wild teenage years lead to a more tranquil maturity.

In part 2, "Relationships," the essays uncover how alcohol helps or hinders a connection between friends and lovers. Depending on the person, alcohol ranges from an aphrodisiac to a force of destruction. It can be a complex equation, in which adding or subtracting alcohol can tip the balance, altering a relationship's essence or fate.

Culture, addressed in part 3, determines much about our drinking choices, habits, and attitudes. We think we're making our own decisions about what, when, how much, and whether or not to drink, but they are often predetermined by background. If you grew up in a house where drinking was taboo, your own drinking might later be infused with shame. If you were raised in surroundings where drinking was celebratory, you might have a carefree attitude about pouring yourself a nightly glass. Daily, occasionally, rarely, or not at all. Beer, wine, scotch, Manischewitz, or gin. Culture plays its part.

And let's not forget about family, discussed in part 4. We love them, dread them, imitate them, are embarrassed by them, run away from them, and often come back home to them. Whether we are following or rejecting our parents' lifestyle, paving the way for our children and other future drinkers, or redefining habits of aging parents, the fact remains that family plays a huge role in our attitude toward drinking.

The book culminates with part 5, "Revelations," in which writers explore the fine line between the transcendent and the dependent. Between the floating and the stumbling, the buzz and the hangover. Alcohol can transport us to a better place or divert us from our path, forcing us to make a crash landing. In the end, we are left to our own devices to define the role drinking plays in our lives.

If there is one theme that runs through this book, it is that—for so many women—drinking carries an emotional charge. It is loaded. Not necessarily bad, but loaded still. The stories in this book testify to the varied relationships women have with alcohol. As two women who have questioned the impact of drinking on our lives, we felt compelled to start the Drinking Diaries story project—from blog to book—by sharing our own. Then we asked other women for stories. And out they came.

PART 1 GIRLHOOD

CANDY IS DANDY, BUT LIQUOR IS QUICKER

"Like most women, I remember my first drink in tender minutiae."
—Koren Zailckas, *Smashed: Story of a Drunken Girlhood*

EIGHT WRECKED CARS AND ONE THAT GOT AWAY

PAM HOUSTON

1.

It is a couple of years after we move from the house with the breezeway in Trenton to the house with the good sledding hill in Bethlehem, which makes me something like six. A warm summer night, driving back across the state line after visiting the Sullivans in the old Jersey neighborhood. Crickets, gin and tonics, the *whoosh* of a new can of Planters Mixed Nuts opened for dinner because if you have six kids like the Sullivans do, the plan is almost always to let them fend for themselves.

Dark night, no moon, windows open in the Caddy (white with chocolate brown interior), smell of honeysuckle in the air. I'm stretched out full length across the back seat—seat belts never a consideration in those days—while my parents murmur softly about all the money the Sullivans have that we don't. My father's old-man eyelids blink like a turtle's—drooping, drooping. Hard to imagine how he sees through the slits.

Then silence, call of a hawk or a screech owl, some night bird out hunting, and all of a sudden I am tossed onto the floor of the back seat and then bouncing; six, seven, eight times, hard off the hump in the middle of the floor. Sharp smell of corn dust filling the air. Snap of the stalks as the Caddy lurches over one last row and finally settles ten rows deep in the cornfield, engine stalling, spitting steam, then ticking, and my father, with such conviction in his voice that my mother doesn't dare challenge him, saying, "Did you see that? The road just ended! The road just ended! Right in front of my eyes!"

2.

This one happens at the first light we come to, right after leaving the Church of the Nativity parking lot. My mother is on the altar guild, which is good on the one hand for the obvious soul-saving reasons but bad on the other. She can't stand to pour all that perfectly good (and blessed) leftover wine onto the ground and often guzzles it in the sacristy after the deacon and the altar boys leave.

I am too short to see properly over the dashboard (still a decade before car seats are required), so I don't see the white van—with ENTENMANN's painted in cheerful, swooping letters across the side—blasting through the intersection on a yellow and clipping the right front bumper of my mother's red Plymouth Fury, spinning it around and around until it stops itself against a cluster of poplars on the front lawn of a funeral home. My mother jumps out of the car, screaming, "I'm sorry! I'm sorry!"—a tactical mistake large enough to get her license temporarily suspended and send her to six weeks of driving school to get it back, even though the Nelson-McGoverns, who pulled out behind my mother and saw the entire thing from their Town Car, said it was almost certainly the guy in the bread van's fault.

3.

Christmas Eve Day, 1972. What I can't remember is why my father and I are at the bar in the first place or why my mother isn't with us. My best guess is that we've gone out under the auspices of buying some last-minute Christmas gifts and ended up here, as we often do.

There is something soul killing about a bar at four in the afternoon on Christmas Eve Day; it is possible that this one time puts me off both bars and Christmas forever. But now we are on our way home from the bar. It is dark but not long dark, perhaps 6:00 PM. There is, of course, a freezing rain. There is always a freezing rain on Christmas Eve Day in Bethlehem, Pennsylvania.

When we get on the freeway to drive the short few miles to our exit, the surface is a sheet of glistening black ice. If not for the fourth negroni, my father might have the wherewithal to slow down for the curve of the on-ramp, but now we are sliding sideways before we have even merged, across one lane and then two, onto the shoulder and through the flimsy guardrail and into the center median strip, which slopes down fifteen feet before flattening out again to accommodate the lanes of oncoming traffic. It is this drop, combined with the sharp sideways momentum, that causes the Caddy (this one gold with cream interior) to roll, once and then half again, down the grassy slope and into the oncoming lanes of traffic, tumbling again—one, two, three more rolls, off the side of the highway and into Monocacy Creek.

The fact that it is Christmas Eve becomes the explanation (among the Irish cops on the scene and the ER nurses) for why the Cadillac managed to cross four lanes of holiday traffic without being struck by another vehicle. And why—although the car is caved in completely, with everything from grille to dashboard accordioned to a third of its original size, all four tires shredded, every piece of glass shattered as if someone had taken a sledgehammer to it, and neither of us wearing our seat belts—somehow my father and I got chainsawed out of that mangled heap of high-dollar metal with hardly a scratch. Others in the dying steel town put it down to good old Detroit engineering. "Any other car than a Caddy . . . " they say to this day.

4.

Dawn is breaking over the Pocono Mountains, and I am here to see it because I have been invited to go skiing with the Morgans. There are three sisters: Greta, Anna, and Hilda. And even though Greta is my favorite, and my best friend since second grade, I love them all: the tall American father who looks a little like the father on *The Brady Bunch,* the tiny and tough German mother whose accent sounds like cranky love, the bouncy springer spaniel, and the buff tuxedoed tomcat who keeps his eye on the canary who keeps his eye on the mom while she cooks whole roasted chickens and spaetzle and peas. I don't dare let myself in on how much I wish this family were my family, but everybody knows it, and they let me hang around. Nobody drinks anything in the Morgans' house except whole milk that gets delivered in glass bottles from a local dairy.

This morning we are all piled on top of each other in the back of the big blue station wagon, a heap of ski jackets, fuzzy boots, neck warmers, and girls, recounting recent plot turns on *General Hospital,* to which Mrs. Morgan is addicted (her only vice, she likes to say, and it's true!). She lets us watch it with her every day after school. There's a thermos of hot milk with Hershey's syrup to warm us up when we get to the ski-area parking lot. There are peanut butter and banana sandwiches with the crusts cut off and baggies of Charles Chips and gummy bears, because who wants to spend ski-area prices for a dried-out hamburger anyway?

Not us! We want to race down the mountain a hundred times, chase each other into the trees and back out again, ride the lift, ski between Mr. Morgan's legs, and sing all the verses to "American Pie" on the way home. Nothing ever goes wrong when I am with the Morgans.

But now the wagon follows a big S curve into the foothills, and when it hits a patch of road that's still in shadow, it starts to float across the invisible ice (is it *ever* summer in Pennsylvania?), on course for a moment and then beginning to turn. Mr. Morgan says, "Hang on, girls!" urgently, but not without his usual good cheer, and that is when we start to spin for real, once, twice, three times around, but slowing as we go until the wagon glides to a stop in the six inches of snow on the shoulder, facing backward, where we watch the chain reaction our braking and spinning and the ice have caused: Five cars, two medium-size delivery trucks, one semi, and one bus bound for Niagara Falls all twirl and glance off each other in what feels like slow motion before coming to rest in various illogical positions, scattered across the highway below.

Now people are emerging from their cars slowly, cautiously. The semi driver jogs up to check on us, tells us he used his CB to call the cops, who are on their way. He and Mr. Morgan agree that it's a miracle no one is injured. And now a few cars are threading their way through the obstacle course, continuing their journey, and a few others have pulled over to offer help.

Mr. Morgan tests reverse, and the heavy wagon responds as if nothing has happened. "What do you say, girls, should we get on up to the slopes?"

"Yes! Yes!" we all shout excitedly.

"Don't we have to wait for the police, Jim?" Mrs. Morgan says. Her accent makes his name sound just like the bark of a dog.

"Didn't hit anybody," he says. "Nobody hit us."

"If we wait for the cops," Greta says, "the whole day might be ruined!"

Mr. Morgan shrugs happily, as if it is all out of his hands, and pulls the car around in a giant U onto the highway. We proceed, a little more slowly, toward the mountain and the lifts.

5.

My mother has decided to leave my father. It is the middle of the night, and we are barreling south on I-95, heading somewhere that I think might be Hilton Head. Neither of us believes she is really going to do it—this is not the first time we have been in exactly this config-uration at exactly this hour of the predawn in her baby blue Mustang convertible. But the idea of Hilton Head cheers us up anyway, with its promise of blue-and-white-striped awnings, young men in tennis whites all trying to make the circuit, sophisticated fish sandwiches served on verandas with tall sweating glasses of tea.

My mother has had too much to drink to be driving. She knows it and I know it, but neither of us mentions it, not now or any of the other twenty million times. Instead I concentrate on controlling our car—and the few other cars we pass at this hour—with my mind; controlling the deer that might be thinking about jumping out of the dark woods in front of us; controlling the cops who might notice the way our car sometimes edges across the double yellow line; controlling my mother herself, who has been alternating all night between giddy and weepy.

She has found something in my father's sport coat pocket, and though she tells me nearly everything, much more than at twelve I need to know, she won't for some reason tell me what it is. "It's too awful" is all she will say about it, wiping her eyes and setting her jaw. Given all we have lived through, I can't imagine what could possibly qualify as "too awful" and still fit into the pocket of my father's sport coat. A G-string? A sticky G-string? Ten used condoms? The severed nipple of an exotic dancer?

We pass a cop, and while I am turned backward to see if his lights come on, a German shepherd lopes into the path of the Mustang. My mother (bless her) swerves too hard to the left and the dog is saved, but we are up on two wheels and then *clunk!* Back down on four, with the car now pointing straight into the trees and still moving. Luckily, the trees are young and willing to separate themselves, trunks from tops, as we hurtle down the embankment nose-first. The trees explode like popcorn all around us until the ground levels out into a muddy clearing and the car shudders to a stop and sinks in.

"You okay, baby?" my mother asks, as she does every time this happens, and then she starts to cry about whatever it is in my father's pocket. I will the cop not to have seen us leave the road, will it to stay dark for a few more hours so my mother can sober up before somebody notices the broken trees, so she won't lose her license and we might, the next time, make it all the way to Hilton Head.

6.

I am in junior high. I am going to guess ninth grade because of what I am wearing, something mother-influenced, most likely Ann Taylor, pin-straight black skirt, black turtleneck, red blazer. On our way home from another altar guild Sunday, stopping at the 7-Eleven for *The New York Times*. It has to be winter because my mother doesn't want to get out of the car and leaves the MG Midget running at the curb while I go in. We are in a hurry to get home before my father gets back from tennis, trying to hide something from him that has to be put away before he gets there, or maybe just to get lunch started and make the kitchen smell promising, a ploy to keep from incurring his daily, irrational wrath.

I reach for the car door, giant first edition tucked under my arm. I slip on the ice and the paper goes flying, individual sections sailing across the parking lot as I hit the ground. My mother reaches across to the passenger side to open the door to see if I am injured and jams her foot on the brake in the process. It's a good thing I'm not lying there, knocked unconscious, half under the car, because what she thinks is the brake is the gas.

The engine inside the little car roars, and I watch from my knees, half the *Times* recollected in my arms, while the roadster hops the curb, picks up the mechanical horse you put a dime in for a one-minute ride, and shoves it all the way to the back of the store. It explodes spectacularly into the vast soda cooler, leaving a topography of Pop-Tarts, Jet-Puffed marshmallows, Cup O' Noodles, and Dinty Moore beef stew in its wake.

7.

I am with my friend Sally on the way home from a frat party at Lehigh University. We are only juniors in high school, but Sally has her license, and we are such good girls—study nerds even—that no one, least of all our parents, would think to look for us at the Beta Theta Pi house on a snowy Friday night.

Sally has the family car, a taupe and wood Country Squire. I can't say how much we've been drinking (a little eggnog punch made with grain alcohol out of a trash can, perhaps?). It does not feel like either one of us is significantly drunk. But there is that black-ice factor again, the rapid approach of Sally's curfew (she has one; I don't), and therefore the imprudent speed at which we are traveling along the wintry expressway. And then there is the jackknifed semi across both lanes and our astonished faces when Sally hits the brakes and the car only seems to hurl itself forward faster. My hands are on the dashboard and hers are at 10 and 2 on the steering wheel, just the way the drivers' ed teacher, who is always trying to get us to give him head while he steers around the serpentine course, has taught us (this will be on the test!). And then the moment when we must duck, simultaneously, as the nose of the wagon slips under the rig, the windshield shattering and the metal shrieking as the bottom of the tractor-trailer peels back the roof of the Country Squire. And then everything comes to a smoky, snub-nosed halt, and Sally and I are blinking at each other with glass shards in our hair, already thanking whatever god it is that protects teenagers from their own stupidity. And the officer later saying, "Any other vehicle than that old battle-ax and we'd be putting you in body bags right about now."

8.

We are driving to Florida for the days between Christmas and New Year in the new Cadillac (this one black with burgundy interior), listening to Casey Kasem's long-distance dedications and reading the SOUTH OF THE BORDER signs out loud. Now that I am "of age," as my father likes to say—though my mother and I don't know what he means by this because I am only sixteen and won't be eighteen until halfway through my first year of college—it is my job to bartend for my parents, moving the ice from the cooler to the shaker, pouring the vodka, passing the bottle of vermouth over the top of the shaker without letting more than a fraction of a drop fall in, shaking, pouring, garnishing with olive and cocktail onions, presenting the glasses to my parents, and repeating as often as directed.

My parents would be happy for me to make one for myself—they encourage me, in fact—but the smell of vodka makes me dizzy, and handling the cocktail onions makes me want to puke. Besides, there is so much holiday traffic to control with my mind, I can't afford to be distracted. And anyway, if we get pulled over, I am the one who has to flirt with the cop.

When I see all the brake lights in front of me, I am so sure that my father must see them, too, that at first I don't open my mouth. There is a price to be paid in my family for back-seat driving, a price to be paid for back-seat anything, which makes my job as controller of the road especially hard, because now I also have to will my father to notice the brake lights, or else my mother, because even though she is afraid of him, too, she is more likely than me to let out a "Watch it, there!" A few more seconds go by and he doesn't notice, and she doesn't notice, and there is nothing for me to do but yell, "Brake!" Maybe another second ticks by while my father regains focus and sees the stopped traffic, but too late, and we rear-end the car in front of us so hard that we cause a chain reaction: three more cars hit by the car behind, mostly just fender benders, except for the car in front of us, which no longer has a trunk, and ours, which no longer has a functioning engine.

"Jesus H. Christ. Why didn't you say something sooner?" my father says while my mother tries unsuccessfully to jam the vodka bottle into the glove compartment even though anyone could see it is four inches too long. I take it from her hand and stuff it into my Bad Company backpack, along with the olives and onions, roll down the windows, and pour out the last of the drinks, waiting to talk to the policeman whose siren we can hear now, racing up the shoulder toward us.

9.

Senior year of high school, nearly graduation. Greta, Anna, and I are headed for the mall on a warm Saturday in May. The girls have been given the retired family car, the big blue station wagon we've been riding in the back of for years.

"You couldn't hurt that thing if you ran it head-on into an oak tree," Mr. Morgan says when he presents Greta with the keys. But it turns out he is wrong, because that is exactly what we *do* do that Saturday afternoon—no black ice, no alcohol. Inattention and inexperience our only excuse.

I don't remember how we get into the middle of the spring green field. (Are we doubled over, as we often are, shrieking and giggling? Am I the one, as I often am, who is making Greta laugh so hard she can't even steer?) And I don't remember why, out of all the places the car could come to rest in that field, it heads straight for the giant oak tree. As if it knows its useful life is over and now it wants to rust away right in that meadow, with the largest tree in the country appearing to grow right out of its hood.

I only remember the look on Greta's face when she calls Mr. Morgan from the farmhouse on the corner (pure sadness, not a hint of terror), and I remember the smile on his face as he strides across the field toward us, opens his arms to embrace her, and says, "I am so very grateful that you are all okay."

RUM-SOAKED

LEAH ODZE EPSTEIN

AT MY SIXTH BIRTHDAY party, my mother got drunk.

We had recently moved to a new house, a new town, a new school, so I invited all the girls in my class to the party. I planned for weeks and even had my mom style my hair in two curly pigtails like my idol, Cindy Brady, whose family was imperfectly perfect enough to fake me into believing they were real. All I ever wanted was a *Brady Bunch* family. The Bradys had one problem per episode, which by the end was neatly resolved. Unfortunately, that wasn't how it happened in my house, where my mother's problems persisted, and grew from day to day.

There we were at my birthday party, all ten of us, sitting around the dining room table in our fancy dresses as my father lit the candles on my cake. My mom had bought it at her favorite bakery. Fancy and expensive, the Black Forest cake had shiny maraschino cherries floating on top of whipped cream sprinkled with chocolate shavings.

I was too young to articulate or understand how embarrassed I was by my mother's outfit, but years later I still remember every detail: the beaded Indian headband—not one of those preppy Pappagallo hair bands so popular at the time, but one that stretched across her forehead. The denim shirt, open so you could practically see her boobs. The bell-bottoms, popular in *Vogue* but not among the housewives of suburban Bethesda, Maryland, where we lived. My mom's straight, dyed-blond pageboy cut set her off from the other moms, who all wore their hair in short poufs. And she wasn't "momish." She was thin—too thin—from the many packs of cigarettes she smoked each day.

My mother stood over me and then stepped up on her chair and climbed onto the table. "Happy birthday to you," she sang, waving her arms like a conductor. I opened my mouth to say something, darting a glance at my friends, and then closed it again, trying to make myself small. My new classmates, eyes pointed upward, mouths barely moving, sang along, practically in a whisper.

When Lauren, queen bee of the prissy, perfect girls, bit into her slice of Black Forest cake, her mouth turned down at the corners. *What could be wrong?* I wondered.

"Ewww!" she said.

Her pronouncement spread like a chorus as the girls at the table all tasted my birthday cake and then mashed it silently with their forks.

My father, as puzzled as I was, since my mother had bought the cake, took a bite and set his fork down in disbelief. "There's rum in the cake!" he announced.

"Don't be ridiculous," my mother said, savoring her slice. "It's cooked in."

I ate my slice, trying to pretend it tasted good, but the cake was unmistakably rum-soaked.

I noted the nervous smiles and darting glances of the moms when they picked their daughters up at the end of the party and my father greeted them at the door. *Where's the mother?* they must have been wondering. Luckily, my father had enough sense to send my mother to their bedroom to "sleep it off." I pictured the girls telling their parents about the terrible birthday party, the weird mom, the disgusting cake.

Before that day, I'd felt lots of things regarding my mother's drinking. When I was three, four, and five, my jumble of confused emotions came out in the form of dizzy spells, headaches, and fears that kept me up all night.

Up until my sixth birthday party, my mother's drinking was our family's secret (or so I thought). Afterward, in my mind everyone knew, and would tell anyone who didn't know, that I came from a "bad" family—the polar opposite of the *Brady Bunch* family, the only other family I believed I intimately knew. And that's when I started to feel something else altogether: shame.

After my party, I developed a dread of my birthday and birthday parties in general. One time, I was invited to a party for a girl up the street. I headed out the door in my fancy dress, but instead of going, I hid in the bushes next to our house for a few hours before coming home. I didn't want to trouble my mother with my worries and fears, so I rode it out alone. I can't remember if the birthday girl's mother called our house to say I wasn't there. (Things were looser in the 1970s, and roaming freely around the neighborhood was the norm.) All I know is that for the duration of that party, I hid.

Eventually, my mother's drinking—her irrational behavior, her sorrow, her rage—got so bad that my father had to padlock her liquor in a trunk. Finally, after he threatened to leave her, my mother went to the hospital to detox and dry out.

The problem was that even after my mother stopped drinking, things were hard for her. Harder, actually. It wasn't like her whole personality magically changed once she gave up the drink. She didn't scream and yell as much, or get red in the face or throw things, but she still couldn't seem to manage most things. "I can't take it" became her refrain.

Sometimes she repeated AA slogans around the house, which let me know how shaky she was.

"One day at a time."

"Easy does it."

As fragile as she seemed, I was scared of her and tiptoed around her, nervous that she would start drinking again or embarrass me in front of my friends. She hadn't magically morphed into the typical suburban mom. She still wore a black leather jacket, cursed and smoked, and ranted about the typical American moms.

Without the alcohol to help her cope, things seemed to freak her out even more. Like my birthday. Especially my birthday. For some reason, my sister's birthday didn't come with the same baggage. Maybe because she was older and spent her birthdays with her friends, getting high.

The cake seemed to trigger it. The rum-soaked Black Forest cake had been replaced with my mother's special Swedish cake. My favorite.

I don't remember how old I was when my mother first walked out on my birthday. But I can still replay the entire sequence of events in my head. She started with the best intentions, announcing that she was going to make the cake, shopping for all the ingredients. Not for her that fake American whipped cream in a can, that too-sweet frosting, or those processed cake mixes—everything had to be made from scratch. She stood in the kitchen, whisking and beating and whipping, making the two layers of cake, the vanilla cream for in between, and whipped cream for the top. Next she washed the berries, sliced the bananas, and then started with a circle of strawberries on the outside, working her way in, with blueberries, raspberries, and bananas.

Somewhere along the line, something went wrong. My mother realized she was tired of standing. And then I asked the fateful question: "When will it be ready?"

Maybe my mother saw the expectations in my eyes and worried that she couldn't live up to them. Whatever the reason, my mother threw up her hands and said, "I can't take it anymore." Then she grabbed her car keys and slammed the door behind her. The car screeched out of the driveway. I didn't know where she went, and I never asked—I was conditioned not to ask questions. She was gone for hours, and I was scared. Terrified, actually. What if she really couldn't take it and decided to drive her car off the road?

It's possible that my mother walked out on my birthday only once or twice, but in my memory it happened every year and was always the same. Until my birthday became a cursed event.

Things changed when I went off to college. The best birthday I ever had was the one I spent far from home in Ithaca, New York, where I was in summer school. I lived in a beat-up apartment with no telephone. I had to rely on mail, and I was pleasantly surprised to get a birthday card from my parents, right on the day. How perfect that card was, with its bouquet of flowers on the front. How easy to convey just the right emotion in a card, which was frozen in time and not subject to fluctuations of stress and mood. That night I spent my birthday with new friends. No baggage. Just fun.

I finally figured out the solution to my birthday problem: As long as I stayed far away from home, birthdays could be okay. Even good. But my mother longed to spend my birthdays with me. She kept wanting to make it right.

When I grew older and had kids of my own, my parents traveled the five hours to the suburbs of New York to spend my birthday with me. And it was usually miserable. Not because of what anyone else did or said but because of what I did to myself. In my head. I'd wake up with a feeling of dread and expectations that could never be fulfilled.

In one photo, I'm blowing out the candle on a pile of flan at a neighborhood Mexican restaurant while my parents, my husband, and my children look on. I'm gamely wearing the sombrero they had given me at the campy restaurant, but I look like a sullen teenager, wishing everyone around me, including the roving mariachi band, would disappear and leave me the hell alone.

"I hate my birthday," I'd say to friends if it ever came up in conversation. It never occurred to me to plan something nice for myself. I'd just wait till someone else suggested something and then follow along—a perpetual child.

One year, long after I'd lain on a therapist's couch three times a week, read *The Dance of Anger: A Woman's Guide to Changing the*

Patterns of Intimate Relationships, and vented my unconstructive rage at all my family members, I decided to hell with it—I was going to ask for what I wanted. The cake. My mother's Swedish cake, without the drama and the walking out.

As soon as I called my mother, I started to regret it. I could hear my own voice and it sounded small, like a child's—even though I was nearly forty at the time. They don't call us adult children for nothing.

I listened on the phone as my mother drew in her breath and sighed. Was it a burden for her to make the cake or was she sighing with relief that I'd finally asked again after all these years? Maybe she was tired of feeling guilty for her past behavior, even if that burden was partially self-imposed. She'd been bending over backward for years to make it up to me, ever since she got sober when I was nine. That's a lot of years of penance.

"Yes. Of course I'll make you the cake," she said. "Anything for my little angel." She was unable to say no, but I feared there would be a cost—to her and to me.

Later, after I hung up the phone, I talked myself through it. *What's the worst that can happen? My mother and I are separated by hundreds of miles. She's older and she's mellowed. She knows her limits. She'll make the cake alone, in peace—without my expectant puppy face—and then she'll bring it up to me when she and my father visit us for my birthday weekend.*

I wondered if I should call her back and tell her not to worry, that I would make the cake myself, that it would be fun for me and the kids to learn. Maybe she could just give me the recipe. But what if she really wanted to make the cake?

It'll be okay, I told myself. *I'm an adult now, and I have my own home, far away from hers. I want my children to taste that cake, to know how delicious it is.*

Maybe some part of me wanted to resurrect the good parts of my childhood, to remind myself that, despite the crappiness, there was sweetness there. What I'd forgotten was that, even though my mother had walked out on my birthday every year—or maybe it just seemed that way—eventually she'd pull herself together and come home, make the cake, and we'd eat it. Delicious.

I told my kids about the cake. "You're going to love it," I said. "Just wait till you taste it." Amazing how I hadn't lost my capacity for excitement and hope. And then the worry set in: *What if they don't like it? What if she doesn't make it after all?* All the old disappointments. The shame.

My mother pulled through and showed up with the cake. She beamed when she placed it on my kitchen counter and carefully pulled the plastic off the top. The kids oohed and ahhed, but when they heard me draw in my breath, and when they saw the look in my eyes, my nine-year-old—ever observant and sensitized to my emotions—said, "It's just a cake, Mom."

"This one's special," I insisted.

It looked exactly as I remembered it, with perfect circles of raspberries—extra raspberries because my mom knew how much I loved them. I would have been happy just staring at that cake, but my mother insisted on cutting me a slice. The first slice, because I was the birthday girl. Or I would be the following day. I decided that we'd eat the cake the day before my actual birthday because that way it wasn't so damn loaded.

The kids got their pieces, took bites, and mashed them around, just like the girls at my sixth birthday party. My kids didn't say "mmm" either, even though this time there wasn't any rum inside.

"They're used to everything having so much sugar," my mother said. "Americans always overload the sugar—they like everything too sweet."

I nodded and bit into the cake. Yes, my kids were used to frosting made with mounds of confectioner's sugar, not a Swedish version with a more subtle whipped cream, with a touch of vanilla extract and sugar, plus the tart flavor of lemon peel.

My mother watched as I took the bite. I expected nirvana, remembering the cake's sweet sponginess, light as air. But the cake was dry, and the whipped cream wasn't as sweet as I remembered.

"I didn't want to add too much sugar, so I cut the amount in half." *Aha!*

"You shouldn't change things," I snapped, immediately wishing I could retract the words when I saw my mother's mouth slip into a frown. "Sorry," I said quickly, wanting to mop up her disappointment.

"I appreciate that you made me the cake. And it's delicious," I said, pushing down my own disappointment and producing a smile. My children were watching, and I thought about how they didn't like it—how let down they probably felt after all the hype about the cake.

I was so busy monitoring everyone else's emotions that I had trouble feeling my own. "Once an alcoholic, always an alcoholic," my mother was fond of saying. And I knew, in that moment, what she meant. *Once the daughter of an alcoholic, always the daughter of an alcoholic.*

Birthdays will always be tough for me—they're all about expectations and hope, and being the center of attention, which goes counter to everything I learned as the daughter of an alcoholic: Don't get your hopes up or you might get hurt. Staying out of the way is safest; make yourself invisible. Don't ask for anything. Don't stress your mother out—she might drink. Don't cause problems for your mother—she has enough as it is.

I remember hearing that addicts are emotionally stunted, stuck at the age when they first started using. I think the same might be true for the daughter of an addict. Every year on my birthday, part of me is still sitting at that table, waiting for my slice of cake with a pit in my stomach.

The memories of my sixth birthday party, and the birthdays that followed, are powerful—so powerful they're lodged in my body. What function they serve, I'm not yet sure. They're not superfluous; otherwise I would just cut them out. Neither are they like the candles on my cake, memories whose burn I can simply extinguish. They're more like the rum. Cooked in, but still the taste remains. Like that cake, I'm rum-soaked. And maybe—just maybe—I'm okay with that, because just like the rum was part of that cake, *daughter of an alcoholic* is part of me.

FOREVER THIRTEEN

SUSAN HENDERSON

WHEN I DREAM, I TEND to return to my junior high. I am forever thirteen—the scrawny kid with the long, knotted hair. And I'm
drunk. I walk the tilted hallways looking for my classroom, not entirely sure what period it is. My shoulders bump into lockers and students, who shout out the words they wrote in my yearbook: "Moron.
Keep your eyes open. Yay for alcoholics!"

The drinking usually starts on the way to the bus stop and continues between classes. I keep a suntan lotion bottle in my purse, and
it's filled with the rum or bourbon I steal from my friends' parents'
liquor cabinets. My parents, nondrinkers, keep only the weird variety
of alcohol that you might add to a fruitcake or cheese fondue. I stand
behind an open locker and my purse strap slips to my elbow as I press
a stream into my mouth. It always tastes a little bit like coconut.

I hold the rum on my tongue until it tingles, feel the slow burn
as I swallow. It blasts first through my nose, then singes its way down
my esophagus until all that's left is the sweet perfume lingering in the
back of my throat. With each sip, my world becomes smaller, like a
fogged-up car—no view beyond the windows. This is what I want, to
feel sealed off from the world around me, focused only on the exquisite taste and the heaviness in my hands.

My friends are here in the dream, their voices echoing like kids
shouting in an indoor pool. I've known most of them since elementary
school, and they are now beautiful and curvy, smelling of Love's Baby

Soft perfume. I look like a child in their company, always a few steps behind them like some weirdo stalker.

Lockers click open and bang shut, and there's the startling bell that tells us to get to class. Now I'm rushing down the hallway, but my gut knows I'm not hurrying to class so much as I'm trying to outrun something that's closing in from behind. I'm just speeding up when I'm yanked by the hair. I feel the pull at my scalp, hear the mad scissoring, and when I turn around, one of my friends is holding a foot-long section of my hair. The laughter echoes as if my head has slipped underwater. I don't have to look at their faces to know that it's my so-called friends who are laughing. I simply keep walking, never saying a word.

Thirteen is the year I like to forget. If I go to a movie in my dreams, it's always *My Bloody Valentine*. The movie's just let out, and the glee we felt sneaking into an R-rated movie and passing a bottle of Jim Beam up and down our aisle of seats has been replaced by nervousness. We all chew gum to cover up the smell of alcohol. Now is the time to sober up quickly, to squeeze Visine drops into our bloodshot eyes, to speak without slurring.

My friends have told me to wait on the curb while they find the older brother who promised to drive us all home. I'm shivering, staring into the headlights in the parking lot, wobbling on and off the curb to stay warm. Finally a car pulls up and honks. I walk up to it and jiggle the handle of the back door and then the front, both locked. I look into the faces of my friends as they laugh, wait for the joke to end and for someone to open a door, but they speed away. For almost an hour, I believe they'll return for me. Eventually, chilled to the bone and thankfully almost sober, I call home for a ride.

There were adults in my life, and it's easy to think they should have noticed this misery, but the truth is, when someone asked how I was, I answered, "Fine."

"How's school?"

"Fine."

"How was your night out with your friends?"

"Fine."

I just didn't know how to open up. Only once, instead of answering, "Fine," did I tell my parents I felt sad and different. My father thought I was being dramatic, and my mother was quick to tell me I was smart and pretty. Of course I had friends, she pointed out, because I spent my weekends with them. Speaking up made me feel silly. It was simpler to keep my thoughts to myself and just continue tagging along with the same crowd, though that choice proved increasingly dangerous.

In one dream, I return to the Smithsonian Mall. It's the Fourth of July, and I'm drinking Jack Daniel's as I move through the huge crowd with my friends. The music is terrible—the Beach Boys long past their prime and singing off-key. A few twentysomethings whistle and call us over to sample beer, brownies, and wine coolers. I have always liked the protective barrier of alcohol, but this is different. I feel as if I'm locked inside a kaleidoscope—my body turning in one direction, the ground in another. Somewhere deep inside I start to panic, but that part soon spins away, as do the hours, and suddenly it's nighttime.

I lose my bearings and most of the friends I've come with, including the one who arranged our ride home. The three of us who are left decide to hitchhike. We take a ride from a guy in his truck, drunk himself. I sit in the cab with him while my friends sit in the bed of the pickup. I don't see it coming, his bearded face so close to mine, trying to kiss me. I freeze and keep my lips pressed shut as I feel wet slime across my mouth. *If I don't move, he'll stop,* I think. *If I don't move, I'm not really here.* He pulls into a clearing in the middle of nowhere, and after he orders us out of the truck, he throws glass bottles at us from his window. I don't know how we get home, but my dad is furious that I've lost my shoes. It's easier to talk about shoes.

I have to wonder why I keep going back to that year in my dreams. Thirteen is just the beginning of my slide. The remainder of junior high is a blur of humiliation, blackouts, and chest pain.

I fall away from my crowd, every one of them, which means I also lose access to their liquor cabinets. The only alcohol left in my life is the stuff reserved for fruitcake and crème de menthe pie. And when those bottles are empty, I finish off the mouthwash in the back of the bathroom closet. Soon there is nothing more to drink, no more protective barrier between me and the world. I am forced to quit cold turkey, though my body protests as I kneel beside the toilet with my cheek against the cold seat, sweating, shaking, and vomiting foam.

"Yay for alcoholics!" No wonder I'm alone. Who wants to be friends with a girl whose hair has slipped into the toilet bowl, who can't leave the house sober, who follows around the very people she wants to stab to death?

Behind the closed door of my childhood bedroom, I can see my hidden self, reading Dylan Thomas poems. I fantasize about meeting him in a bar and talking all night, snow falling outside the windows. In that small room, I'm a good dancer, play air guitar, wail along to black gospel on Howard University radio, and write papers that aren't due in any class; I just want to write them. I'm fierce, emotional, opinionated, and alive. But I leave that authentic, vibrant person at home, afraid to risk being different.

Somehow, I find a best friend in the high school janitor, of all people—a fellow poet who sits with me at the back table of the cafeteria with a little cassette deck between us that plays Jessye Norman arias. He teaches me how to put my hidden thoughts on the page and make them sing.

I also meet a boy who writes me notes and, after school, gives me rides home, where we listen to records and do crossword puzzles together. It takes him almost a year to kiss me, something that teaches me a great deal about trust.

I start to raise my hand in class, sharing the opinions I used to keep to myself. My first attempts at speaking out loud are embarrassing—my voice squeaks and the words come out in a jumble. But over time I get so comfortable with talking in class that I sometimes have to sit on my hands to give others room to speak. There are countless twists and surprises.

I have to believe I visit my thirteen-year-old self at night for a reason. I have spent a lifetime berating myself with the words scribbled in my yearbook, but maybe the most telling comments are the ones that appear over and over: "Sorry I never got to know you but have a great summer." Looking at thirteen from the safe distance of my forties, free from the fear that I'll spend my life drunk and unloved, I can see the real tragedy is that no one knew the person I was in private. Because it was only when I showed my hidden side in public that I found true friends and a life full of such beauty that I wouldn't dream of blunting it with a drink.

LIVING THE DRY LIFE, ON CAMPUS

ANNA KLENKE

IT'S ONE OF THE FIRST things they tell you on the admissions tour. Right on the leafy sidewalk between the administration building and the student union, it pops out: "We're a dry campus!" The nicely dressed, backward-walking tour guide smiles and makes eye contact with the parents in the group, while the prospective students shift uneasily. *A dry campus? How do you have fun on the weekends? Doesn't everybody go to college to drink?*

Sometimes it did seem like everybody went to college to drink, even on a campus that had supposedly banned alcohol from its premises. St. Olaf College, a small liberal arts school in Minnesota, has been dry since it was founded by Lutheran, Norwegian immigrants in 1874. Despite this conservative heritage, my "dry" college was no different from a state university in many respects—house parties, beer pong tournaments, and recycling bins overflowing with liquor bottles were the norm on most weekends.

The difference was the amount of effort we had to exert to hide our alcohol use. At St. Olaf, you had to be clever. One guy famously tried to sneak a case of beer into the dorm by claiming that the square bulge under his sweatshirt was a tumor; water bottles often turned out to hold straight vodka; and I once saw a girl use a syringe to inject rum into a juice box.

While I never actively agreed with the alcohol policy, it didn't affect my life much during my first two years at college. My friends didn't drink, and I didn't have much experience with alcohol, so I mostly ignored the issue. By my junior year, however, things had changed. Most of my friends drank regularly, I turned twenty-one, and I also became an RA. This meant that I was expected to enforce the alcohol policy, potentially getting my friends and classmates in trouble if I caught them with booze. All of a sudden, the dry campus became a bigger deal than I ever expected.

"RA on duty!" The words squeaked from my throat as I banged my fist on the door to be heard above the pounding bass. "Could you please open the door?"

Someone cut the music. I could hear bottles clinking and people whispering as they stashed the alcohol in closets and drawers. Two full minutes passed before an enormous football player cracked open the door. "What?"

I clutched the bright green duty binder, my one pathetic marker of authority. "It sounds like you have a party going on in there," I said. "Can I come into the room?"

"Sure," the football player said. He swung the door wide open. Nine or ten sophomores stood around a folding card table loaded with red plastic cups. They were all taller than I was and obviously drunk. "We're playing water pong," he said. He shoved a cup under my nose. "Want to smell it?"

There was water in the cup, but the room reeked of beer. I put on my best one-of-the-guys face. "Okay," I said. "Seriously. I heard bottles clinking when you turned off the music, and I can smell booze. I know there's alcohol in the room. Could you just make this easier and bring it out?" I hoped my tone was friendly but firm, like they had taught us in RA training. It was probably more wobbly and weak.

The whole crowd stared at me stone-faced. "I don't know what you're talking about," the hulking linebacker said, looming over me. "It's just water pong."

"Yeah, quit trying to bust us," one girl in the back murmured.

I spied a mini-fridge in the corner. "Could you open the fridge?" I asked.

He opened it. A gallon of milk, cheese, a jar of pickles. This guy was good.

"Okay," I said, feeling like the lamest person to ever walk the halls of a St. Olaf dorm. "Just keep the music down. It's almost quiet hours."

As soon as the door closed behind me, they all burst out laughing. I bolted for the elevator, shamed once again, the tiny RA who didn't have the gumption to enforce the alcohol policy effectively.

The problem was that I didn't follow the alcohol policy myself. The St. Olaf student handbook states: "The possession, distribution or consumption of alcoholic beverages is prohibited on the St. Olaf campus, on land owned by the college, and in college-owned honor and language houses." Once I turned twenty-one, I had a hard time accepting that my school had the right to tell me not to drink. I tried to imbibe mostly off campus, but on a few memorable occasions, a friend hosted a dorm room party that was too good to resist, so I broke the rules.

The consequence for an RA's getting caught with alcohol on campus was loss of position, which carried with it a whole host of larger consequences, such as housing reassignment, reduction of scholarship money, and death by parental rage. So, naturally, the first thing I did at any party was scope out the nearest closet into which I could climb if we happened to get busted.

The second thing I did was to warn everybody in the room that I couldn't get caught and that I would leave if things got too loud. I would then pour a drink into a camouflaged container and spend the rest of the night whipping my head around to look over my shoulder as people went in and out of the room. Buzzkill? Yes. But I was too busy being paranoid to worry about my social standing.

During my junior year, some friends hosted a fall festival in their room. It was a great theme party and included activities like pumpkin carving and bobbing for apples—both of which are way more fun when you're intoxicated. I drank too much vodka and grapefruit juice, accused my best friend's boyfriend of not liking me, and took some truly hideous pictures, which of course ended up on Facebook, before stumbling home. It was the first time I had come back to the dorm drunk, and figuring out how to use the elevator took some time. So did finding my room and unlocking my door. Luckily, I didn't run into any of my residents. Even three sheets to the wind, I knew that a drunken RA is not a reliable RA—the last thing I wanted to do was start making sloppy declarations of eternal friendship to my residents. Half an hour later, when I needed to throw up, I was too scared to go to the bathroom for fear I would be seen or heard. And that's how I ended up on the floor in my underwear, puking into a trash can and tearing up over the fact that I was such a bad role model. I never came home that drunk again.

Halloween rolled around two weeks later. Everyone was more excited than usual because Halloween fell on the night daylight saving time ended, allowing an extra hour for drunken debauchery and an entire Sunday for hangover recovery. It was also the first weekend after fall break, so the campus was ready for a big welcome-back party. Students began drinking early in the day and wore their costumes to "drinner" (drunk dinner) in the cafeteria. My RA staff had decided to put three people on duty that night to deal with the shenanigans that would inevitably go down. I wasn't on duty but came home early from a party that had gotten too loud. So I was able to watch the ambulances drive past, lights flashing, as more and more students went too far. We had nine people transported to the hospital for alcohol poisoning that night. One of them was abandoned, unconscious, and lying on the dorm room floor incapacitated until the RAs found him. The college across the river, which is not a dry campus, sent only three students to the hospital that night.

That night really made me see how futile a dry campus is. The administration seemed to enjoy pretending that alcohol wasn't a problem at our small Christian school, but it was. Students obviously still drink on a dry campus. They also drink more dangerously. I've seen friends down eight or nine shots in succession before heading out onto campus for a dance or a concert. What could be an evening of slow, more relaxed drinking turns into a rush to get as drunk as possible before leaving the safety of your dorm room, even for students who are twenty-one.

The college used to provide a shuttle (known by students as the drunk bus) between the campus and downtown on Friday and Saturday nights, but it discontinued this service, forcing drunk students to drive or walk the mile back to campus. A few times a year, the entire student body received an email informing us of a reported assault late at night. Many of the attacks involved alcohol in some way.

While I had mixed feelings about the relationship many of my peers had with alcohol, the most difficult thing for me was to enforce a drinking policy that I adamantly disagreed with. Unfortunately, it was an unavoidable and complicated part of my job. I know there were plenty of parties I wasn't invited to because of my RA position, and I know that many residents viewed our entire staff with suspicion, thinking we were all out to get them. At staff meetings we joked about buying a Voldemort mask to wear around the dorm, just to drive the point home.

Because of my occasional policy violations, I worried constantly about getting busted and being exposed as the Worst RA Ever. I went to great lengths to hide my lone bottle of vodka at the bottom of my smelly laundry basket, despite the fact that I lived in a single room and locked it religiously. Once, I ran into a resident while I was drinking on campus and spent the next week terrified that he would rat me out. I even had to untag pictures of myself on Facebook in case someone from residence life saw them and figured out that I had been at an on-campus party. I regret the amount of time I wasted worrying about drinking and obsessing over the alcohol policy, and it makes me sad that the dry-campus policy stigmatizes drinking, even for those who are of age. The zero-tolerance attitude adopted by some schools functions only to make the drinking culture a secret—and consequently makes it more difficult for students to get help with alcohol problems if they need it.

During my last week as a residence life staff member, I got called on an alcohol "medical," which is RA-speak for when someone goes on a bender and needs an ambulance. The guy wasn't a student at St. Olaf but was visiting his girlfriend, who lived down the hall from me. She called the paramedics when he passed out and took care of him until they arrived, holding herself together. When they carried her boyfriend away on a stretcher, however, she lost control and started sobbing. I can't imagine having to watch someone I loved in that condition: vomiting, eyes rolling back, incoherent. It was traumatizing for me, and I had never seen the guy before in my life.

I wish there was a six-week course or an informational video that could illustrate the not-so-glamorous side of college drinking that I got up close and personal with during my two years as an RA, but nothing can simulate the "Oh my god, *really?*" feeling that comes with discovering surprise vomit in your bathroom when you are stone sober. That's just something that everyone needs to experience for themselves.

I'm sure the prospective students touring St. Olaf's beautiful campus right now are having their college party fantasies ruined by some smiley tour guide proclaiming the wonders of the dry campus. They shouldn't worry too much. The liquor store is only a mile away, and there are plenty of upperclassmen willing to provide innocent freshmen with their first "real" college experience, hangovers and all. The newbies will find out soon enough that college isn't just about drinking—there are, after all, concerts to attend, video game competitions to enter, sports to play, and possibly books to open. While some students choose alcohol as their number-one college activity, most people I knew had a lot more going on in their lives than the contents of their secret booze stashes. As an RA and professional party pooper, I may not have had the "typical" college experience, but I am happy with my choices. I had a lot of fun, watched my friend drink a juice box filled with rum, and stayed out of the hospital—all while living the (mostly) dry life.

MY FLASK

PRISCILLA WARNER

LOOKING BACK, I WAS so self-conscious about my turquoise polyester uniform that it's no wonder I suffered my first panic attack behind the grease-splattered serving counters of the Brown University cafeteria. I was a fifteen-year-old "Ratty Queen."

Back in 1968, Brown's cafeteria was officially named the Refectory—the Ratty for short. Who knows which witty Brown boy dreamed up the nickname Ratty Queen? In any case, it was no worse than "townie," which is what I was—a local Providence girl who took a menial job for a chance to meet, or at least stare at, an Ivy League prince.

My friends and I attended an all-girls high school, and the thought of surrounding ourselves with college boys was thrilling. We were too old to go to summer camp, too young to get real jobs, and bored with the beaches of southern Rhode Island. So when an older schoolmate told us about a short-term waitressing gig at Brown, we were intrigued. Six of us were hired to work for one month, until college students would take over our jobs. Although we barely cleared the dishes in our own homes, we happily served up lunch and dinner in the Brown cafeteria.

While the school uniform I wore every day was a shapeless green plaid skirt and sweater, my waitress uniform was tight through the bust. I imagined a future with one of the hundreds of boys who passed by my station: tall ones, short ones, blonds, jocks, preppies, hippies, science nerds. There were very few women around to compete with us Ratty Queens—at the time, they all attended Brown's sister school, Pembroke, which had its own cafeteria. So as my co-workers and I dished out mystery meat, the boys were all ours. I gawked at them, pretending to myself, and to them, not to care.

But of course I did care. I cared desperately. My ninth-grade diary of a trip to France with my French class is fifty-three pages long and contains 108 references to boy watching or boy craving. "I wanna meet a guy so bad," I wrote. My main focus that summer was how, exactly, the girls in my group managed to talk to and make out with boys while I stood there tongue-tied.

Back home in Providence, I'd stare into my bedroom mirror every night, parting my lips and smiling at myself ever so slightly, desperately trying to look carefree. I must have known I would never truly be carefree. Even before my panic attacks began.

And they began with a bang.

As I stood behind the serving counter at the Brown cafeteria, dishing out peas to an endless line of boys, I felt an electrical current tear through my body. My heart raced, skipped beats, and flopped around in my chest. My lungs tightened up so fast that I couldn't breathe. Or so I thought.

I was actually breathing too quickly. I began to hyperventilate. My throat closed up, my body trembled, my arms grew rigid, and my fingertips tingled. I thought I was dying.

I managed to stagger back to the kitchen, call my house, and plead for a ride home, where I curled up in my parents' bed. I watched, dazed, as a family physician paid a house call, examined me, and announced that I was "just a little bit nervous."

Just a little?

The doctor wrote me a prescription for Librium, and I joined the ranks of the unhappy housewives who were stoned out on tranquilizers like Miltown and pretending to enjoy their lucky lives.

But was I lucky?

I lived in a huge house with an intact family (although my parents fought regularly, and mental illness ran through the family like wildfire). I had many wonderful friends (although none of them ever seemed to panic like I did). I drove a cool car (an old Jaguar my grandmother had given me when she moved to Florida), and I got good grades. (I never hyperventilated once on the premises of my high school. The sunny yellow buildings provided a calm counterpoint to the psychedelic interiors of my house.)

It's hard to be the only sane person in a household. Or the only insane one. And in the chaotic confines of my adolescence, I was never sure which person I was.

But I was sure of one thing. I needed an ally in my battle against panic, and the grown-ups didn't seem to be reliable or strong. But they had access to something that was: alcohol. Vodka, to be specific.

Vodka is colorless and odorless, or so I'd been told by friends during clandestine trips to local package stores. If I was going to rely on alcohol to keep me sane and normal, no one could ever know that I felt insane and freakish.

And no one could know that I needed vodka by my side at all hours of the day and night, just in case a panic attack snuck up and clobbered me, which it did regularly—at my new job as a supermarket cashier, at pajama parties at friends' houses, at the movies, at the beach, even. I needed easy access to an emergency stash.

It's not that I wanted to get high. What I wanted from alcohol was to slow down. Whenever I took a gulp, a warm, fiery sensation traveled down my throat into my lungs, bathing them in a warm glow. They stopped convulsing and carrying on. Vodka slayed the dragon I couldn't slay on my own.

The tranquilizers I'd been prescribed didn't work as quickly as my secret stash did; liquor was indeed quicker. But I needed to devise an efficient delivery system, available at all hours of the day and night.

I needed a flask.

A bottle of Valium was easy to conceal in a pocketbook, but I couldn't carry around a pint of vodka. Nowadays you can buy flasks in many shapes and sizes, made of all sorts of material, including sterling silver. But I bought my flask in 1968, and it wasn't even really a flask. I think it was actually a hot water bottle from a drugstore. It was plastic, white, and bulky, and eventually it turned dingy, rusty, and scratched.

It was way too big, but I made it work. The cheap vodka I poured into it made a sloshing sound as I lugged it around in my purse— *glug, glug, glug.* I didn't care how it sounded as long as nobody saw it was there.

I took my secret flask everywhere—walking around town, in cars, on planes, trains, and sailboats, on dates, and later, when I went off to college and beyond, to classrooms, on job interviews, and into ladies' rooms. A swig here, a swig there—whenever I felt a panic attack coming on, I took a gulp of what I considered to be magic medicine. For years, the fiery liquid distracted me from what was raging in my central nervous system. Although I would have been mortified if anyone had ever seen the flask I carried with me everywhere, it was comforting to know that I had two weapons in my arsenal against anxiety—Valium, the new drug I'd been prescribed, and my dear old friend, vodka.

They were a lethal combination; I knew that thanks to the tragic tale of Karen Ann Quinlan, a twenty-one-year-old in New Jersey who had collapsed at a party after drinking alcohol and taking Valium. She lay in a coma for years, a constant reminder to me of the dangerous path I was on. As a result of her cautionary tale, I never mixed alcohol and Valium. But I wanted them both with me at all times.

Until shortly after I graduated from college, when alcohol betrayed me.

My body began to reject the medicine that had soothed me. I was working long hours as an advertising agency art director, buying Folonari Soave by the half gallon. I'd wake up in the middle of the night with a start—my heart pounding. I'd lie in my bed wide-eyed, shivering and shaking. The warm, mellow glow I had relied upon had turned into jolts of all-too-powerful, unwanted energy.

Gradually, I cut back on drinking. I made this decision on my own, even though everyone around me continued consuming.

One copywriter I worked with claimed that she did her best work during lunch hour, which she'd insist we spend at a bar near our office. I'd order club soda, and she'd order three glasses of wine. Sometimes I'd sip a glass to make her feel less self-conscious. But I cringed for her when she'd order a large iced tea to go and bring it back to our office in a paper cup, refilling it all afternoon with wine she kept hidden in her desk drawer.

I'd attend business dinners with my husband and watch executives kick back three quick drinks before they could loosen up. I'd go to parties where I noticed people's behavior shifting with every glass they lifted to their lips—women got giddy, and men became bold.

I didn't judge any of these people. I realized that we were all self-medicating. But while I had no idea what secrets these people might have been hiding, or what issues they were wrestling with, it was clearly time for me to step up and address my own pain.

I became my own sort of holistic physician as I modified my lifestyle. When I experienced panic just before my periods and throughout my pregnancies, I recognized the role that hormones played in my anxiety, and tried to go easy on myself at certain times of the month. Running around on a tennis court left me breathless, so I switched to jogging slowly, which calmed me down. Caffeine made me jittery, so I stayed away from coffee and Diet Coke. And every time I woke up in the middle of the night with a pounding heart, just hours after consuming a few glasses of white wine, my resolve to stay away from alcohol was strengthened.

I'd gotten married to a man who loved me, panic and all. I'd given birth to two wonderful sons, whom I managed to parent while hiding my anxiety as best as I could. I lost my father to cancer, and my mother was diagnosed with Alzheimer's. In other words, life threw me the curveballs everyone must eventually contend with.

I managed to hit singles and doubles, with an occasional home run. I coauthored a best-selling book about religion and toured the country for years on an extended book tour. In the skies above Oklahoma, I opened up a magazine and read a story about Tibetan monks who meditated so effectively that neuroscientists were studying their brains.

I want the brain of a monk, I decided. And monks didn't carry flasks. They lived with a kind of peaceful purposefulness I could only imagine and wanted to attain.

I wrote and sold a book proposal outlining a journey I hoped to take from panic to peace. I attended meditation workshops and learned how to sit still. I met wonderful monks, rabbis, healers, therapists, and mystics, who helped me eventually rewire my shaky brain and mend my frayed nerves. I learned how to self-regulate and to desensitize my body to the panicky feelings that had clobbered me when I was young. I uncovered secrets from my childhood that explained some of my sadness and fears. I learned that suffering is inevitable and that it often comes in waves. But I learned how to be a surfer and how to ride those waves with some confidence.

I confided in a wonderful therapist that despite all my healing, I still carried my latest incarnation of a flask with me everywhere. I showed her the miniature plastic bottle of vodka I'd bought on an airplane years earlier. It was scratched and filthy; the once blue-and-yellow label, Svedka Citronella, was now a dingy gray.

"How long will I continue to carry this around?" I asked her, embarrassed.

"I quit smoking," this therapist confided in me. "And for ten years I carried an old pack of Camels with me everywhere, with just three dusty cigarettes inside. You'll carry what you need to carry until you won't anymore, one day."

My family and I flew to Detroit to attend a cousin's graduation at the University of Michigan. One hundred thousand people flocked to the giant football stadium to hear President Barack Obama deliver a commencement address, and security was tight. It had been announced in advance that no one could carry a backpack or pocketbook, so I shoved my ersatz flask—my miniature bottle of vodka—and some cash into the front pocket of my jeans.

A metal detector went off as I trailed behind my husband and sons, who were barreling into the stadium. Busted, I turned my dingy bottle, with its banged-up metal screw top, over to the authorities. My husband chuckled; my sons barely noticed. I sat inside the stadium naked, with one hundred thousand people around me, stripped of my security blanket.

But I stayed calm.

I bought another miniature bottle of vodka at the airport before we flew home. It sits at the bottom of my purse to this day, reminding me of my frailty, taunting me just a little bit. I'm not cured. I'm not totally enlightened. I'm not as brave as I'd like to be or as weak as I once was. The bulky, plastic drugstore "flask" of my youth seems comically out of place in the emotionally healthy life I've managed to build for myself. But on some days, I'm still an ex–Ratty Queen from Providence, left occasionally breathless at what life can be and become.

PART 2 RELATIONSHIPS

HERE'S TO US!

I like to have a martini,
Two at the very most.
After three I'm under the table,
after four I'm under my host.

—Dorothy Parker

THE DAYS OF WINE AND SELTZER

BY ELISSA SCHAPPELL

WHEN I PICTURE MY favorite moments with my husband, someone is always holding a glass, or a bottle of wine, or a plastic cup. I can plot the timeline of our relationship by what we're drinking.

The first: a Bloody Mary in a can I bought for us to share on the Amtrak train, where we'd just met. The cold Rolling Rocks we drank the next night, on our first date, at a bar called Downtown Beirut on the Lower East Side. The glasses of Pernod on the rocks we sipped while listening to the Velvet Underground after I moved in with him (and his three actor roommates) on Staten Island. The coveted one-hundred-year-old armagnac that my father—clearly drunk with happiness that his daughter had finally brought home a man he approved of—decided to break out and share with Rob.

Historically, any time my family gathered together, there were always bottles of wine. The empties rolled across the floor to honor those who couldn't be with us and to celebrate the fact that we were all together. Home for the holidays in Delaware, there were shots of aquavit with oysters on Christmas morning. There were always after-dinner drinks—chartreuse and port and whatever exotic liquors my parents might have discovered on one of their trips to Czechoslovakia or Rangoon. The summer we joined Rob's father in Aspen (as Rob had done for years), there were daiquiris and oil can–size containers of Foster's Ale for the family's traditional sunset parties on the terrace.

There were the icy martinis we'd toss back while I worked as a reporter at *Spy* magazine and Rob worked in the magazine's research department, a river of gin that connected us to the past and our heroes of the Algonquin Round Table. We wore linen and drank gin and tonics barefoot in the grass at our wedding shower. On our honeymoon in Portugal, there were tall glasses of passion fruit juice mixed with absinthe. The next year, fired up by the history of great expat artists living and creating abroad, we picked up and moved to Portugal, where we drank white bootleg absinthe to the point of hallucination. We drank drafts of beer that we bought for pennies in East Berlin. There were countless glasses of wine: retsina in Greece, chianti in Italy, sancerre in France, gewürztraminer in Germany, port and *vinho verde* in Portugal, which we bought in plastic casks that you brought in for a refill.

Back in a series of New York dives, there were scores of champagne bottles, magnums, and jeroboams; hundreds of champagne flutes toasting the weddings of friends and family, the birth of our children, the weekend, the memory of those who couldn't be with us. There were hundreds of cold beers and cheap bottles of wine drunk on the roofs of apartment buildings while we watched the sunset with our friends, discussing the role of art in society and why Sebadoh would never make a better record than Pavement.

Alcohol was the fuel, the catalyst for our artistic ambitions, as well as the social lubricant that helped us find others who also burned like Kerouac's roman candles. In those days, dinner parties sometimes ended with our jumping in the car and driving to Atlantic City, Niagara Falls, or—one New Year's Eve—cross-country. Trips I'm not sure we'd have taken were we not all in the bag and that I'd regret never having made.

There was the sangria we made every year for our traditional spring party, a drunken debauch that raged until the wee hours and always—until our children were somewhat cognizant—resulted in guests sleeping over. There was hot chocolate with schnapps we drank in a ski house on the slopes of Steamboat Springs, waiting out a blizzard. There was god-awful but terribly cheap Great Wall of China plum wine, as well as ironically consumed fifths of Night Train and Thunderbird. There was the gallon of Famous Grouse I'd bought for Rob when I got pregnant, which by the end of the second trimester was gone. The chartreuse reserve that we shared with my family after my daughter was born and when my father was dying.

We met when we were twenty-one and married at twenty-three, so we were the one couple all our friends seemed to know—the ones you crashed with when you moved to New York or broke up with your boyfriend. Our sofa was always occupied, and our guests' glasses were never empty.

There were, of course, the hangovers. Mornings when we'd wake up late, stumble to an East Village diner for something greasy and restorative, then trundle home to collapse on the sofa, felled by the cocktail flu, giving us permission to watch basketball doubleheaders, eat pizza, and doze all day long in each other's arms, getting up only to be ill.

It wasn't all pleasant—there were fights, broken glasses, thrown shoes, mornings after when I couldn't recall exactly how the night had ended. Had I been an angel or atrocious? And I'd have to turn sheepishly toward Rob—who no matter how blotto he'd been (and for the record, the man could, should the situation warrant, appear sober as a judge) never seemed to forget anything—and try to gauge by his face how badly I'd behaved. "I'll never drink again," I'd say, spouting the classic sober atonement.

Perhaps it should've been me who stopped drinking. But instead Rob was the one who quit—eleven years ago, nearly halfway into our twenty-three years together. I don't remember the last bottle of wine we shared, the last shot or cocktail. I do recall that the last time he drank was at our spring party in 2000. Our daughter was four, and my father was dead. Rob had just taken up bike racing, having been a competitive runner in college. Riding twenty miles a day was, I'm pretty sure, all that kept him from murdering us in our sleep.

I confess: I hoped he'd start drinking again. I'd never thought he had a problem with alcohol (which perhaps speaks more to my relationship with alcohol). I missed him playing Nick to my Nora Charles.

I wasn't alone in my wish. I became acutely aware of how Rob's new status—an island of sobriety in a sea of inebriation—made some people uncomfortable. Old friends didn't know what to make of this turnaround. Why wasn't Rob drinking? Had he kicked the sauce completely? Was he judging them for drinking? Should they dial back their boozing? Was he an alcoholic?

Die-hard boozers shuddered at the sight of him sipping a seltzer, as though giving up drinking was akin to his moving to Amish Country. He was lost to them. You know, if Rob was an alcoholic, maybe they were, too. And that tedious prospect—AA meetings, crawling up the twelve steps, making amends—wasn't happening. If he was serious about bike racing, it made sense that he'd stop drinking or taper off—during race season. But to just give it up? In a community not known for its commitment to fitness of any sort, giving up drinking for a sport was unheard of.

Perhaps it would've made more sense to everyone if Rob told people he'd "quit" drinking—*quit* being a word freighted with drama and implying addiction—versus "given up" drinking, which suggests a willing sacrifice. While he did think he was drinking too much before he quit, he never really feared becoming an alcoholic—which left him in a sort of no-man's-land. If he had a drinking problem and started going to meetings, he'd have met a whole new group of friends. You can't throw a rock in New York City without hitting an artist in recovery. But it simply wasn't the case.

For his part, the sober Rob is quieter, less garrulous, less interested in staying up until three in the morning debating whether Mark Kostabi was a genius or a con man. Why is Lou Reed such an asshole? If you were born with a tail, would you keep it or have it surgically removed? When folks want to head off to the pub to grab a couple beers and shoot the shit, he rarely joins them. He doesn't do it with me, either.

Which doesn't mean he's opposed. More often than not, my husband will ask if I'd like a glass of wine when we're out for dinner and might even request a taste if it's particularly good. He sees that I'm kept in Maker's Mark and hard cider.

However, I'm not inclined to drink that much when it's just the two of us. I know I could drink all the gin martinis I like, and Rob would toss the olives in the air for me to catch in my mouth like a trained seal. Still, it can make me self-conscious. Plus, nothing makes one feel quite as "stupid drunk" as trying to carry on a smart conversation with a sober person—misunderstanding simple commands and questions, continually dropping your end of the conversation like a sofa you're attempting to maneuver up a flight of stairs. It's ridiculous and potentially dangerous. Drinking is simply not as much fun as it used to be when we were in it together.

I miss the intimacy and attentiveness that sharing a bottle of hot sake demands, as neither is allowed to pour his or her own cup. Drinking alone—enjoying a glass of wine or a scotch by yourself while reading, or in the tub, or late at night watching it snow—is a lovely thing. But sitting and drinking a bottle of wine by yourself in the afternoon or even at dinnertime? It can just make you feel more alone.

I have great respect for Rob's decision to stop drinking. Moreover, I admire his quiet and steady dedication to his bike training. Now that we have kids, I appreciate that they are growing up in a home where one parent drinks and the other doesn't. It demonstrates to them that drinking is a choice, not a requirement. That while drinking can be an enormous pleasure for some, it can be the downfall of others.

Our days of wild drinking were very much tied into a time and place—primarily downtown New York in our twenties and into our thirties—when we were finding ourselves, our circle of friends, our voices as creative people. It is hard not to be nostalgic for that time, for that sense of endless wonder and opportunity and adventure. So what if our car breaks down in a blizzard in Colorado while driving cross-country?

Now, with careers and kids, those years seem far away. With Rob not drinking, a bridge to that past is also gone. And yet, if the light is right and I'm holding a nice glass of Cloudy Bay, Rob's ubiquitous seltzer looks like the old gin and tonics he used to drink. All our real-world pressures fade away, and it feels like anything is once again possible.

MY FIRST SOBER KISS

ADRIENNE EDENBURN-MACQUEEN

"CAN I KISS YOU?" he asked. The question from my coworker had been hanging in the air for weeks, and I should have been ready.

If this were a movie, I'd have smiled sexily and leaned in. Or I'd have said a breathless *yes,* my answer perfectly crafted by a Hollywood screenwriter, leading to the hottest sex anyone has ever had.

But this was real life, and there was a full minute of silence as I hesitated. We were not lounging on satin sheets, bathed in a rosy glow. No, we were in sleeping bags in a shitty little cabin, our housing courtesy of the volunteer program we belonged to. I was covered in mosquito bites and poison oak and sweating profusely. He was not offering me a glass of champagne. Or a shot of vodka. Or a shot of anything.

This was real life, and I was stone-cold sober.

I was twenty-three years old, and I'd never kissed anyone sober. The full weight of this realization threatened to ruin an already awkward moment. The silent seconds grew heavier until I answered his question with a shrug and replied, "I don't know."

Three years have passed since that night, and it still makes me cringe to remember my answer. At twenty-three I had already kissed a small army's worth of fellows. I'd let a good portion go much farther than that. I'd started young and kept a steady pace, and I'd done it all without any of the hesitation and awkwardness that threatened to ruin the aforementioned encounter. Because I'd been drunk.

One might think (as I incorrectly did) that quitting is the hardest part of recovery. The choice I made to quit drinking as a depressed and physically obliterated twenty-one-year-old came easy. It took weeks of staying home and crying all day for me to realize the significant difference between not drinking and living sober. Every day I discovered new things I was excluded from. The frivolous things that I'd always loved, like wedding toasts, tailgating, and beer pong, eventually became things I could enjoy sober. (Most people don't mind drinking double during beer pong, and I never lose my depth perception.) However, as I approach my twenty-sixth birthday and nearly four years without alcohol, I have compiled an ever-growing list of significant things that I miss, things that would be better if I were a responsible drinker.

Every year, on the anniversary of our mother's death, my sisters have the option of easing their pain with a drink or five. I listen to the shitty folk music my mother loved and try to find solace in the fact that she would be proud of me. As I get older, my peers are beginning to have a more mature relationship with alcohol. They are brewing their own beer or developing a palate for expensive wine. Now I find myself at adult parties where instead of getting wasted and throwing up in my purse, I try to feign interest when people discuss infusions and aged whiskeys and debate the purity of tequila. I have pretended to care during many wine tastings. I try not to look too awkward as I sit drinking Diet Coke, reminding myself why it was a good choice to quit and resisting the urge to go home and put myself into a coma with a $9 bottle of vodka.

But topping the list of significant things that would be better if I were a responsible drinker is dating. Dating while sober is often an embarrassing and ruthlessly un-fun experience. I never learned how to flirt well or interpret signals. Though I have no problem going to a bar, a lot of people find it hard to comfortably drink around me. I don't even have the basic relationship knowledge that most people gain through growing up, and not just because I started drinking in my early teens. I had no boundaries or concern for anything. By the time I was fifteen, I had a voracious drug and alcohol habit, and I was also a world-class slut.

It doesn't take an advanced degree in psychology to understand how I turned out the way I did. I was one of those babies parents pray for. I had a wide, sunny smile, bright green eyes, and adorable chubby legs; I had curly red hair, the kind that strangers stopped to marvel at. "She should be in magazines," people would tell my parents, and it was true. A decade later those comments were brought to a halt as my awkward stage was ushered in, triggering a deep-seated self-hatred and humiliation that would have long-lasting results. My smile was covered in wires and elastics, and my constant squinting finally gave away the fact that my pretty green eyes couldn't see a damn thing without glasses. The fine red curls turned into a tangled, frizzy mess. The only thing that stayed was the chubbiness.

I knew other parents who went out of their way to help improve their children's appearance, but mine were busy. My mother found a lump in her breast when I was eleven, and from then on my parents didn't notice that I was ugly and fat. They didn't see that I was hiding behind my glasses and refusing to smile. Disease has a way of forcing people to rethink everything, and by my parents' new definition, I was beautiful simply because I was healthy.

Like all phases, I outgrew this one. By the time I was thirteen, I looked fairly normal again. My braces came off. I grew six inches. I got contacts. I was introduced to hair serum at summer camp. I even made friends I didn't secretly hate, including the two I would come to rely on for booze and drugs over the next ten years.

Alcohol made everything easier. I was charming and fun, and lots of young men found my wild behavior and carefree attitude appealing. In hindsight, it's clear they were attracted to the fact that I was easy. I spent most of my teenage years giving the proverbial milk away for free because I still felt like the ugly preteen I had been, a feeling that only drinking and affection could quiet. It was a long time before finding me attractive wasn't my only prerequisite for a potential suitor.

Before the age of eighteen, I had lost my virginity to a boy whose name I still don't know, slept with dozens of others, and cheated on the few guys who were dumb enough to think I was girlfriend material—all under the influence of alcohol. There were times when I did engage in sexual activities with only a few drinks running through my system, but only with someone I had previously hooked up with while blacked out. I was a sophomore in high school when I drunkenly participated in my first threesome, and a senior when a doctor told me that my awful cramps and heavy bleeding weren't a cyst, as my mother thought, but a miscarriage. "I didn't know," I told my astonished parents, because it was the truth. "I was being careful." Which was not true. They weren't angry, just sad. I think we were all relieved that what would have been a heartbreaking decision had been made for me. On the way home from the hospital, we cracked jokes to ease the tension. I laughed along with my mother, grateful not to be in trouble. I didn't know then that she'd never be a grandmother, that within four months she'd be dead and that alcohol would soon be the only thing that could fill the hole she left in me.

By my high school graduation, I had developed a reputation. Painkillers and cocaine joined alcohol as staples in my diet. They were the only things I truly loved. I didn't give a fuck about the countless men I involved myself with, and I certainly didn't care about myself. My friends and I laughed at my attitude toward romance; they were jealous that I could be so unattached, and I was grateful that no one could see through my act.

In the midst of my haze, I found a good man. We had a relationship based on love but built and fortified by nightly drinking. For two years, we sat next to each other on barstools, slurring *I love you*'s and clumsily planning a future. Despite my deep feelings for him, he became a crutch that allowed my addictions to blossom. I was hopelessly dependent and developed the ugly and unfair habit of blaming him for my stalled future. I was faithful for over a year before I cheated on him, an awful incident that both of us managed to believe was caused by whiskey. He should have broken up with me. I should have realized that my dependence on alcohol was sabotaging every part of my life. Instead, we moved in together and drank more.

A few weeks before I turned twenty-two, I found myself in handcuffs, having managed to climb out of the wreckage of a van I'd flipped. The arrest didn't convince me that I had a problem; nor did everyone's shock that I'd extracted myself from the wreck unscathed. For many, simply knowing that they could have died (and probably should have, according to the police) would have been a wake-up call. But I was so far gone that I didn't care. It took two weeks of blackout drinking before I woke up to the first honest thought I had had in years: *I don't want to die.*

Alcohol had been my companion since childhood, and I was crippled without it. Drinking had exacerbated my worst attributes, but it hadn't created them. The spineless girl who cheated and lied was me. The hurtful words and destructive thoughts were mine. I was emboldened when inebriated, but the potential to be destructive always existed deep within me.

The next year was a pride-crushing experiment in creating a new life. I slowly became a person I didn't hate, someone who was honest because it was right and not just convenient. I no longer allowed for things like coincidence. Everything is caused by something, and I was responsible for my pathetic life. It grew monumentally less pathetic when I realized I needed to handle the blame for what had become of my life.

I was astounded by how much my boyfriend loved me. His own drinking was never a problem, but he was more than supportive of my decision to quit. He loved me when I was a drunk teenager, and he loved me as I slowly became a sober adult. But it wasn't enough. I broke up with him because I wanted a new life.

Within minutes of ending my relationship, I realized I was fucked. I was twenty-three, and single, and didn't know how to talk to a guy without consuming at least twelve beers first. I quickly found out that there is no attractive way to explain why you can't accept a free drink from a stranger. Because I am so young, most people don't assume that I am an alcoholic. Instead, they think I am seriously religious or taking medication. My least favorite thing is people's assumption that I'm pregnant. I don't miss the days of waking up with no recollection of how I ended up in a stranger's bed or the feeling of vaguely recognizing someone without knowing why.

What I do miss are the risks that alcohol allowed me to take. Now I can't pretend that what I do is anything but a clearheaded decision, and my fear of humiliation often holds me back, making me appear bored, shy, or dim-witted. It took months before I saw any sign of progress. I felt inexperienced, not in kissing but in being vulnerable to the possibility of rejection and embarrassment without a single drop of alcohol to lessen the intensity.

Like everything else, my first sober kiss was not perfect.

Having so much built-up anxiety, I was relieved to find that I hadn't lost the ability to make out. The surprise was finding out how ordinary it is. I had pictured some secret euphoria, something I missed because I was mostly unconscious during my formative years. I imagined every touch would burn. We'd orgasm in a cataclysmic simultaneous explosion, fall deeply in love, and live forever without fighting, aging, or having to pay bills. Instead, we bumped teeth and noses. He knelt on my hand and my shirt got momentarily stuck in my mouth as he pulled it over my head. I tried not to focus on the unremarkable and slightly gross sounds of two people trying to suck each other's face off.

As we tumbled around, I analyzed what I was doing, strictly following the mental checklist of a dance that, though fuzzy, I did know well. I stretched a hand down, purposefully trailing it over his pants. When I reached for his zipper, however, he stopped me. My cheeks burned when he informed me there was no rush. I felt chastised and slutty, utterly humiliated. Another girl might have been reassured, but instead of seeing his confidence in a next time as honorable and romantic, I was completely ashamed that he might be questioning why he had respect for a girl who obviously didn't deserve it. As I pulled away, he continued kissing me. His desire to move slowly wasn't a harsh judgment. He was just letting me know his limits.

In focusing on my previously reckless behavior, I had ignored the fact that I was used to being disposable. I was always just something to fuck when the bar closed, a fair judgment made not by chauvinist pigs but by men who gave me the exact amount of regard that I required from them: none.

Mine, despite what it seems, is not a cautionary tale. I've spent almost four years without a drink, becoming a person I've come to like. Though it would have been easy enough to amputate my former self from the person I am today, I made a conscious decision not to. Very few of my old friends stuck with me through my sobriety, so the majority of my friends know me only as a logical and responsible adult. They would be ignorant of who I used to be if I didn't insist on remembering her. I spent too many years buried in disgrace, caused not by alcohol, as it might appear, but by a deep-rooted lack of self-worth. I cultivated my current self-esteem with outright honesty, a bold decision to go through life wide open and genuine. The blemishes and bruises that could be interpreted as weaknesses instead remind me that I can take a hit without shattering. I didn't die in that car. It would be a sure and shameful mistake to bury my old self as though I had.

Because this is a true story, there is no fairy-tale ending. We do not ride together into the sunset. My first sober kiss was simply a realization about my own self-worth—the only lasting part of that encounter. When I woke up next to my coworker in the morning, still mostly clothed, I felt the old rush of regret and disappointment, but only for a second. He opened his eyes, and I saw that he was happy to be waking up next to me. He pulled me closer, half-asleep, and for the first time in my life, I didn't feel like someone's drunken mistake.

THE SWEET SMELL OF EXCESS

SARI BOTTON

AL-ANON SUCKED. If I hadn't been too broke for therapy, I'd never have taken a friend's advice to attend those awful meetings. They were worse than the AA meetings I'd been to over the years in support of my string of alcoholic boyfriends—three, if you're keeping count. The AA people, when they finally hit bottom, were brave, copped to shit, and took responsibility for all the nasty things they'd done when they were drinking. The Al-Anonics were victimy and whiny. Everything was someone else's fault.

The people in Al-Anon were "addict addicts," who needed others in the worst possible way and yet would counterintuitively go for only the most unavailable, most uninterested, meanest people around. I, of course, did not see myself that way—I, who was addicted to alcohol not by mouth but by nose, specifically on the breath of a difficult man.

Joey, my friend in AA, suggested I try his meetings instead.

"I'm not an alcoholic," I pointed out.

"Here's what you do," he said. "Lock yourself in a room with a case of Jack Daniel's and don't come out until it's all gone. Then go directly to AA."

I thought about it. While I was at it, I might try writing, too. I'd always wanted to try writing drunk. I imagined it would free me from my crippling, good-girl inhibitions.

I couldn't, though. I'd sworn off drinking nearly four years before, ostensibly for holistic health reasons. But also for a guy named

Matt. I kept my vow of sobriety as I moved on to Jimmy, and then to Michael. How on earth would these poor men stay on the wagon without my selfless support?

That right there is what kept me hooked. How vital I imagined I was to another's well-being. What power I could have. All while appearing saintly and superior. Trade that in for the occasional glass of wine? No way. This was much more intoxicating.

Except the buzz never lasted long. In a matter of time, each boyfriend would return to drinking, and I'd feel like a failure for my inability to prevent that. The relationship would bust apart—sometimes for a while, sometimes for good.

MICHAEL AND I WENT back and forth a few times over the years. Of all my men, Michael had the hardest time staying sober, and I had the hardest time walking away from him. A long-haired musician with handsome features, he was always surrounded by women and had difficulty being faithful. He reminded me of my grandfather, the original drunk in my life, alternately affectionate and icy, and unfaithful to my grandmother.

Pappa could put away a fifth of Johnnie Walker Red a day. I knew this because I worked for him at his Seventh Avenue sportswear business. When my cousins heard I'd started working there, they joked, "What do you do, pour scotch all day?" That *was* one of my jobs. It started at 10:30 AM. He'd ask me to wash a glass, grab some ice, and pour some Johnnie. I did that over and over until it was time to catch the train home to Long Island.

I knew that smooth, perfumey, malty smell so well. I had been inhaling it since I first sat on Pappa's lap as a little girl. It simultaneously tantalized and lulled me. Michael's breath was infused with vodka rather than scotch, but it worked.

My last go-round with Michael, beginning in the fall of 2000, could have been avoided. It'd been five years since I'd seen him, and in my mind, whatever appeal he had—the powerful sway he once held over me—was long gone. I thought I'd finally learned my lesson. But it turned out I had overestimated my recovery from this particular addiction.

WE MADE PLANS ON the phone to meet at his band practice in a rehearsal space off Sixth Avenue in the West Thirties. His deep baritone voice had previously bemused me, but now it came with the memory of the way he'd get by the end of most nights—the verbal nastiness followed by incoherence, followed by his nodding off mid-sentence after so many beers and vodka shots. Not to mention the memory of his hitting me. It was hard to believe I ever wanted to be anywhere near that.

I didn't even think of the sex, the amazing sex, Michael's specialty. It eventually fell by the wayside anyway. Every time we'd get together again, the sex would be there for a while, and it would be *good*. He knew how to make me feel just the right combination of beautiful, special, sexy—even if I saw myself as a mousy good girl. Probably because I was a mousy good girl. But once the sex wasn't new anymore, his drinking would pick up. He'd lose interest and eventually switch his focus to another fawning fan of his band, another mousy good girl desperate to catch a glimpse of her inner sexpot in the mirror of Michael's flattering attentions.

I was getting together with Michael that night, I honestly believed, to clear the air after so many years of silence following a fight we'd had. I'd gotten sick of his shit and moved on to someone else, and he had hung up on me. I figured five years had passed. We'd known each other since we were kids. We had close friends in common. Enough already.

Okay, maybe I was also interested in trying on—and showing off—the mantle of just how over him I was. I was thirty-five and, yes, on the rebound from a relationship with *another* alcoholic—one not nearly as far gone as Michael.

The attraction/repulsion ratio shifted the tiniest bit inside the rehearsal space. I was put off by the sight of the forty-ounce Budweiser Michael swigged at every break, in every song. The man was thirty-seven now. He came from Upper East Side affluence. Time to stop posing as a kid from the streets of Chicago, where he went to college. Realizing he was still stuck in that groove made me feel sorry for him. In that detail alone there was danger for me.

He smiled the warmest, most welcoming smile when I entered the studio. It was probably the nicest reception I'd gotten from him in the more than twenty years I'd known him. I felt something inside me, my resolve maybe, loosen and resettle at a slightly different angle.

Remarkably, despite his continued drinking, Michael looked good. He still had some of his summer tan. He was fit—an indication that he was likely still rising at five most mornings to get on his exercise bike and sweat out the rest of the booze from the night before. He still wore his black, corkscrew hair long. It swung back and forth each time he rocked on his feet to the music. He caught my eye, once, twice, again, again, smiling warmly each time, and that's when I started to feel it: *the love.*

In that moment I was of the opinion that it was a friendly love, the innocent love of acceptance and mutual forgiveness between two old friends who met as teens and were something like siblings before becoming lovers.

One potent ingredient of that love was pity. Unfortunately, that night I didn't recognize what a slippery slope that presented for me. It was a key component of my attachment to one beautiful mess after another, this feeling sorry for them. It nudged me to absolve them of all responsibility and opened the door for me to wrest control. It was a subtle, unspoken transaction. My internal superhero emerged from the shadows to earn credit for saving them, whether or not they wished to be saved. Often they stated their preference not to be, which had the opposite of the desired effect: I only became more insistent. *Do not try to stop me.*

Even though I was feeling warmly toward Michael at the rehearsal space, I still thought I was safe. But then we went—where else?—to a bar in his neighborhood. I was not drinking, a habit I still maintained post-Jimmy. I'd assigned myself the role of the non-drinker girlfriend to drinker boyfriends, apparently even when I no longer had a boyfriend.

At the bar, Michael drank one glass of house white after another. He said he'd recently replaced vodka with wine, to good effect—he didn't get completely blotto. That was something he'd figured out after an unsuccessful stint in rehab.

A strange thing happened. Michael told me about the girlfriend he was involved with when he went to rehab—Sheila, a drug and alcohol counselor who had driven him to the rehab facility in the lush hills of the Hudson Valley and then dutifully showed up to get him at the end of his stay with the can of Foster's he'd requested. As he relayed this story, Michael became visibly and audibly tipsy. He pronounced a few words just slightly incorrectly. His eyelids got heavier. As he got drunker, I got illogically, emotionally intoxicated myself—most likely a by-product of my competitive feelings toward Sheila. *She brought him beer after his time in rehab? Amateur!* I could do so much better. I could really save him, cure him of his addiction, given the chance. A tragic, codependent drug and alcohol counselor was no match for me and my virtue, my selfless love, my uniquely, magically medicinal vagina.

Michael must have noticed this shift taking place in me, because he made his move. He took hold of my hand across the table. He gave me another of those smiles, and then we went back to his apartment. What was one night for old time's sake?

In the morning, Michael's stale white-wine breath filled the room and turned my stomach. I found the presence of mind to tell him (and myself) that more of this kind of thing would be a bad idea, especially if he was still drinking. He looked wounded, and as flattering as I found that, I was pretty resolved.

Whew, I thought when I left. *Dodged that bullet.*

But days later he did what I always thought I'd hoped he'd do: He begged.

"I need to do this—I need to get sober for you," he pleaded, and I was nauseated.

"But they say it never works when you get sober *for* someone," I reasoned. I also instinctively knew that he wasn't ready, and I doubted he ever would be. There were too many other women around him who were eager to make transactions similar to mine, to let him do whatever he wanted in exchange for his making them feel important and powerful, too.

"Please?"

He was serious.

"And promise you won't leave me if I fall off the wagon? Promise to stick around and help me back on?"

Holy shit. He was truly recognizing my great power. What he was requesting was the opposite of the much advised tough love. But fuck that. I was so in.

Things were great for a few weeks. Michael was eager to try, and he replaced his fixation on alcohol with a fixation on me. He wrote me songs, wrote love letters thanking me for being the only one courageous enough to insist he stop drinking. Michael was sober, and I was higher than a kite, strung out on his intense adoration.

But right on schedule, he fell off the wagon. Hard. He'd never made it longer than a month, and we were rounding three weeks. Just in time, his last girlfriend, Sheila, the drug and alcohol counselor, sent him a Christmas card. He met her for a "friendly dinner." He called me that night and tried to hide his slurring.

"I can't talk to you like this," I said.

"But you promised you wouldn't leave me if I fell. You said you'd stay and help me get up."

I did. I went to Al-Anon, bristling as people whined. When Michael stopped going to AA, I dragged him there myself, holding his hand the whole time. After meetings, he'd sneak off. He always had to be somewhere. I knew where. In 2000, cell phones were not yet ubiquitous; Michael called from pay phones, and the names of the bars they were situated in came up on my caller ID. They were often bars in Sheila's neighborhood.

Michael's drinking got worse—so bad that he passed out as we were eating dinner at a Thai restaurant in Midtown, snoring with his head on the table as people tried not to stare.

Suddenly I was the enemy. "At least Sheila will drink with me," he argued on the phone one evening. "You're. No. Fun." He had this way of punctuating his words when he was sloshed, in what seemed like an effort not to sound that way. "If you'd just come with me to the bar . . . " He fell asleep.

Okay.

I'd go with him to the bar.

Maybe sitting there across from him, sober, I could appeal to him. And get him to go back to AA. And change his ways. And save his life! And save our love! Because I was just that awesome and powerful.

For a guy who clung to the mid-nineties grunge look, Michael had weird taste in bars. He liked these shiny Midtown tourist traps on the ground floors of hotels, which especially appealed to high-class hookers and their businessmen-in-from-out-of-town clientele. One well-dressed flight attendant type came back with three different men in the course of an evening as I sat and watched Michael down seven pints of draft beer, each one followed by a shot of chilled Stoli.

I stared as he pounded, wondering what it felt like inside his brain. I was fascinated by the idea of being blissfully anesthetized but not quite tempted to go there myself. I found myself torn between wanting to be fun like Sheila and wanting to get serious and save Michael. One minute I was laughing at his stupid jokes, positioning myself just so to receive his sloppy, fragrant, vodka-tinged kisses, and the next I was crying, pleading, "When will you be ready to get sober again?"

"This is just a bender, babe," he said, holding me tightly, alcohol fumes wafting from his mouth and off his skin, enveloping me, caressing me. "I just have to go all the way through this to get to the other side. Stay with me. We'll get there."

There was more drinking, more dragging Michael to meetings, after which he would run off. Then the confession.

"I cheated," he admitted.

I punched him in the stomach. I stopped taking his calls.

"What about me?!" he shouted into my answering machine. "I want to kill myself, and you won't even pick up the phone. Would you even cry if I died?"

Whoa. By just answering the phone, I could save his life. But I was tired of being so powerful.

Still, I went back. I should've been done with him the night he grabbed me by the shoulders and shook me, hard. Or the night he grabbed me by the throat in a bar. But it wasn't until the night he canceled our plans so that he could stay at Sheila's and drink that it was finally over for me. (Apparently I was less concerned about bodily harm than I was about injuries to my ego.)

In agony, I decided to try Michael's antidote for that. I needed to know what it was like, what he and Sheila felt when they were knocking back shots. I went to Detour, the jazz bar across the street from my East Village tenement. I hadn't had a vodka drink since my eighteenth birthday, when a single screwdriver yielded bed spins and a terrible hangover. But that night I wanted vodka. I knew the smell. But I wanted to know the taste. It was my chance to finally try writing drunk.

There was a woman about my age singing old standards accompanied by a guitar and bass. I ordered a vodka martini. I liked the way it looked in the glass—clean, simple, all business. After four years with not a drop of alcohol, I sat at the bar and sipped it slowly.

It went right to my head. I felt like I was in a bubble. The edges on the bar sounds softened. Everything moved more slowly.

Once I finished the drink, a man at the end of the bar sent over another. I smiled at him, not feeling the least bit flirtatious or amorous. This stuff made people want to rip each other's clothes off? The appeal was lost on me.

Sip . . . sip . . . sip. I felt out of it. Removed. Numb.

I stumbled back across the street to my apartment. As I lay down on the couch, exhausted, I noticed my journal on the coffee table. This was my chance. Inhibitions be damned.

The next morning I woke up with a crushing headache. The journal was on the floor. I picked it up. There were only two lines: "I drank vodka tonight. I can't feel my face."

IN THE YEAR AFTER we broke up, Michael tried several times to reach me, including on 9/11. He called once after midnight, drunk, from a bar. I hung up on him.

I'd finally had enough of it all, my ridiculous sense of greatness and what it cost me. As painful as that last round with Michael was, I think I needed it to cure me, and to kill my romantic notions. It's now been more than a decade since I've spoken to him. Two years after our ending, I met my husband. Michael was my last alcoholic boyfriend.

According to twelve-step wisdom, you're never fully recovered from an addiction, only forever recovering. Maybe I'm naive, but this time I believe I'm truly, fully recovered.

IT. MUST. BE.

BECKY SHERRICK HARKS

STEF AND I WERE ELEVEN and thirteen, respectively, when we met. It was almost a sort of chemical reaction between us, the kind that occurs once or twice in a lifetime—if you're really lucky. It was like our cells pulled us toward each other. It was clear the universe had plans for us.

Always looking for some fun, we were brought together on a fairly regular basis at this party or that. While I managed to get my drink on without ending up in the bathroom, praying to the porcelain gods, Stef knew no boundaries. Whether at school, where she carefully concealed a fifth of vodka in a bottle of Sprite, or off grounds, where she got obliterated out of her mind on a nightly basis, she knew only excess. As she drank, her eyes sparkled, her pupils wider and wider, threatening to swallow up the green of her iris whole, as though she were seeing a magical, mystical world no one else could see.

We grew up in the same white-bread town, the lawns sprawling and green, the people friendly, the skies a deep blue, the carpool lane full of BMWs and Porsches, the land bisected neatly by a river. The walls of her parents' modest suburban house, a simple seven-minute drive across the river from mine, showcased her life. A photo of baby Stef, giggling and covered in mashed potatoes. Stef wearing zebra-print pants, posing with a gigantic goofy smile, pretending to be deep in conversation with a mannequin. Picture after picture displayed a lifetime of smiles and laughter, a stark contrast with the omnipresent sadness in her eyes, which came later.

Stef was a love child born into a blended family—the result of an affair between neighbors. Her parents then married, raising her alongside her much older siblings, who delighted in tormenting and torturing their baby sister. Through the photos, it was easy to see that despite her siblings' torture, she was a well-loved little girl.

In school orchestra, we were known as the Bad Girls—our heads together, giggling over this or that. It was there, Stef by my side, as we drank deeply from her special bottle of soda—more vodka than soda—that I remember seeing the words for the first time. In his String Quartet no. 16 in F Major, a brilliant piece we once played together, Beethoven had scribbled *"Muss es sein?"* (Must it be?), to which he responded, *"Es muss sein!"* (It must be!).

And that's how I thought of our friendship: *Must it be? It must be!*

Oh, how we laughed, sitting there in the orchestra pit surrounded by our classmates, not quite in on the joke, snorting unladylike through our noses in a moment of unbridled joy at that particular bit of eccentricity. Back and forth we'd joke in our best (worst) German accent, *"Muss es sein?" "Es muss sein!"*

It must be. She must be. I never told her how much I admired the hell out of her. Bracelets jangling handily on her arms, bell-bottoms hugging her hips, a vintage Stones T-shirt—effortlessly thrown together. She was larger than life at age sixteen. The boys wanted to be with her, and the girls wanted to be her. I'd never known anyone like that.

I'd never known anyone who would take my side, either. Every other friend I had would've shoved me under the bus. The betrayals were reminiscent of my lonesome childhood, living as the daughter of two alcoholics who allowed me to raise myself. Alone.

At six, I had more experience being by myself than most people do at twenty-five. I never expected to find someone who gave a shit about me, so when Stef showed up to tell my cheating boyfriend to fuck off or my former friend that she was being a total asshole, I was stunned. It had always been me and me alone. Defending, well, me.

When I discovered at twenty that I'd gotten knocked up by my cheating boyfriend, Stef was the first person I called. I wept into the phone, scared out of my mind, the future a striking black question mark of uncertainty. While everyone else in my life fretted and cried and yelled and blamed, Stef simply stood back, rubbed my growing belly, and sang a silly song about having a baby. When she finished, she said, "Congratulations, Becky. I'm going to throw you a baby shower." And she did. It was perfect. She sat with me day after day as my first son grew inside me. We watched trashy television on her couch. It was such an unexpected kindness in a turbulent, miserable part of my life.

Weeks after I had my son, making her officially Auntie Stef, she found out that she, too, was expecting. We celebrated her pregnancy, but once her child was born, her shine and warmth dissipated until they were only a glimmer. Her sadness overwhelmed her. Stef did the only thing she knew how to do to force that sadness into submission: She drank. Instead of her eyes opening up to that joyful world she once saw, she sank further into her despair. The alcohol couldn't touch that sadness.

I didn't recognize it for what it was—mental illness. Alcoholism. I simply thought that while the rest of us grew up, Stef turned into an overgrown party girl. It had to be something she would snap out of, right? I mean, we'd ditched the all-night parties in favor of cramming for midterms and caring for our babies. She'd certainly do the same.

She didn't. And still we didn't see—couldn't see—what had happened to our brilliantly kind, sparkling friend. She was drowning, and we didn't throw her a raft.

Almost immediately after the birth of her first, Stef accidentally got pregnant again. Although she felt bursts of joy while loving her two young sons, her pregnancies must have triggered a dormant mental illness—maybe it was always there. The addiction, that was certainly always there, too. Must it be? It must be.

Bipolar disorder, they called it the first time she ran away from home, leaving the babies in the care of her very worried mother. Frantically, Stef's mom called me, the police, the homeless shelters, looking for her daughter. When they finally found her hiding in a local shelter, her parents got her into an inpatient psychiatric unit. When I called Stef on the psych ward, she was overjoyed to hear from me.

"They think I have bipolar disorder," she told me in her off-the-cuff manner, like she was giving me the punch line to a joke rather than a serious diagnosis.

I sucked in my breath, trying to steady myself before responding. My own mother is both bipolar and an alcoholic, and hearing that my friend was suffering the same way broke my heart.

"When you get out, we'll catch up and grab some coffee, okay?" I said. I'd already taken off my partying pants and thrown on my parenting pants, so the days of carousing until we had drunken conversations with a lamppost were in the distant past.

When she left the hospital with a pocketful of pills that she swore she'd take (and never did), the partying that had once been a good-natured way to pass the time became her way of life. It shattered me to watch her spiraling downward—closing the bars and rubbing up on random strangers night after night.

It was only then that I realized she was no longer drinking to liven up a dull party. No. At twenty-two, my friend was an alcoholic. I couldn't take it. Too many childhood memories, too much pain, too outside my own comfort zone to handle it. My mother's own alcoholism had forever marred me, and my friend, my precious friend, was headed down the same path. I couldn't watch it. I couldn't even say her name without the gorge rising, the tears close.

I saw her a handful of times after that.

Immediately after the birth of her second son, I visited her at her parents' house, where she was living with her boyfriend and two sons. The person who answered the door looked like my best friend, but she didn't act that way.

Up in my face, just a tad too close for comfort, she hugged me as she greeted me at the door, holding her new son. The words spilled out of her mouth faster and faster, and I struggled to keep up with what she was saying. Manic. She was manic. She was also drunk—the booze seeping out of her pores, nearly choking me. I checked my watch. It was only ten in the morning.

We went out for a girls' lunch, leaving her sons in the care of her boyfriend, and over cheese fries I tried to reach my friend. I tried to tap into who she was, the person I remembered loving so dearly. She was nowhere to be found. She talked over every word I uttered, laughing hysterically at the salt and pepper shakers. Without speaking, her behavior wove a tale of sadness in between her slurred, manic speech and her bloodshot eyes. This was not my friend. I didn't know this person.

That was one of the last times I saw the person my friend had become. After that lunch, I drove home and wept for my friend who was so very lost; her mental illness hit me too close to home, and I knew I had to move on. Stef was lost at the bottom of a bottle of vodka, and not a single one of us who had loved her back when she sparkled and shone could get through to her.

While Stef was in and out of rehab, and in and out of shithole bars, I grew up. I got married, bought a house, and had another baby. I'd taken my life, once in similar shambles, and turned it around. She'd done the opposite. I had two cars and a mortgage. She lived in a homeless shelter. I had two cell phones and a landline. She couldn't afford a working telephone. Our lives had once been so intertwined that I couldn't tell where one of us ended and the other began, and now this. I kept tabs on Stef through her mother, who'd bankrupted herself to send Stef to rehab one last time.

The last time I heard from Stef, the person who'd loved me when no one else had, she left a message on my cell phone. The message was cheerful and upbeat, just a "Howdy, I'm out of rehab. We should catch some coffee. I'll call you back, since I don't have a phone."

Oh, how I wish I'd picked up the phone.

Her mother called me on a sunny February morning, days after I received that last voice mail from Stef. I was beyond chipper to see her number on my caller ID and answered the phone in the brightest voice I could muster on two-year sleep deprivation. I figured it was high time to catch up with my old friend, treat her to a cup of coffee, and tell her that I loved her.

Then her mother said those three words: "Becky, Stef's dead."

I slumped to the floor of my cheerfully lit kitchen. I couldn't breathe. The room, once so full of oxygen, had turned into a vacuum.

For days I pored over flower arrangements, my young son clamoring for my attention as I wept on the couch, not sure what to send to a funeral for someone who simply should not have been dead. Someone who should have been sitting there next to me, laughing at the absurd phrases for the bouquets: "With Greatest Remembrance" and "Deepest Heartfelt Sympathy." Whom would I ask what kind of flowers to buy for someone who had been around this world for only twenty-six short years? Because I sure as hell couldn't pick any. Hours upon hours I spent perusing the websites to find something appropriate. In the end I bought nothing. There was no "I Cannot Believe You're Dead" arrangement, no "But You Have Two Beautiful Sons" spray, no "Please God, Tell Me This Is a Sick Cosmic Joke" casket cover.

Her funeral was standing room only, filled with people whose lives she'd touched without even trying. When the string trio started playing "As Tears Go By," the entire room cried. The delicate floating harmonies of that song were simply too sweet for this occasion. I'd have preferred angry thrash metal, the heavy guitar riffs ripping through the air in the funeral home. Anything but those light notes hanging in the air.

I nearly vomited when I saw her youngest son—his face a mirror of his mother's—lean into the casket, coming up covered with the makeup applied by the mortician to make her look like she wasn't dead. The image of her two sons screaming—dressed in the type of tiny, somber black suit no child should wear—will be forever seared into my brain.

"Mommy!" the boys wailed as the casket was shut.

Age twenty-six, found dead in her bed. Cirrhosis of the liver. Two young sons who would never know the way their mother lit up a room. Gone. Alive one minute, dead the next.

I've spent years agonizing about what I would say to her given the chance. One last conversation. Perhaps I could offer her some meaningless trite bullshit consolation: "My grief has gotten better over time" or "I still miss you, but I'm okay now." But it would be a lie.

It's not better three years later, only different. The gaping hole she left cannot be filled. The world is still a darker place without her. I could tell her that, years later, with the millions of words I've written, almost none is about her. None seems to be enough. They cannot quite capture her essence.

I guess I could tell Stef any of those things if I could have one last conversation with the person who showed me what real love, real friendship, and real loyalty are.

I'D HUG HER ONE LAST time, feel her warmth, bask in her light, and have one last laugh. I know what I'd say to my friend, the right words finally on the tip of my tongue: "Must it be?" "It must be."

RUNNER'S HIGH

EVA TENUTO

WHEN I WAS DRINKING, I was a runner. I did whatever I could to sprint from reality. I developed a sixth sense for partners who were unavailable and felt compelled to pursue them with obsessive gusto. I captured the most inappropriate nonapplicants and used creative, persuasive tactics to get them to apply. The more they tried to get away, the more I tried to hold them hostage.

My last relationship prior to being sober was no different. I ran into the future; he ran from the past. There were rare moments when we were truly in each other's presence. He wasn't a bad person. He was hysterically funny, which won me over. But despite the attributes that made me love him, he was a heroin addict. And despite my best intentions, I was an active alcoholic.

I drank every night and showed up to my teaching job hungover every morning. I loved the kids because, unlike my boss, they didn't notice if I turned up late or with gray teeth from drinking an abundance of red wine the night before. I spent countless nights cruising up and down the Brooklyn-Queens Expressway like I was riding the Cyclone at Coney Island. When I was behind the wheel, one eye open, three lanes appeared as six. I dropped off friends, picked up others, and looked for the after-hours spot the bouncer from the last place had told us about. Every night I made it home was a lucky night.

On our own, my addict boyfriend and I were a mess. When mixed together, we created unnecessary catastrophes. It was like living *Who's Afraid of Virginia Woolf?*. In our last episode, he decided to move back to Jamaica, his native land. I was teaching full-time, had a good job and a nice apartment, and did not want to move. So we broke up. Of course, once we were two thousand miles apart, he suddenly felt more open to a real relationship.

He wanted me to come and visit for my birthday weekend. So I did. When he picked me up at the airport, he looked like he had suffered a terrible flu. He said he was so glad I was there. He was dope sick. He couldn't live like this anymore—the streets were mean to him, and he needed me.

I didn't know about his history of bouncing between places—that every time he moved from New York to Jamaica he'd start using heroin, and every time he moved from Jamaica to New York he was strung out and needed to get clean. All I knew was that for the first time, he was running toward me instead of away, and I wanted it to work. By God, I was going to make it happen.

I couldn't think of a better excuse to take the focus off my own issues. *He* was the one who needed to get better, and I was going to fix him. I didn't want him to die. I wanted to have everything I dreamed of with him, regardless of the mixed messages I had always received. I went into an alcohol-induced frenzy: *If only he had a laptop, things would be okay. That's what I'll do, I will buy him a laptop—then he can start a graphic design business. But wait, how will he meet his clients? I'd better get him a car, too.*

I even persuaded him to try to get me pregnant. I knew it wasn't what he wanted, and considering the state of our relationship and the amount of alcohol I consumed daily, it was not something that I should have wanted. But in the storybooks, don't the trapped men always love the baby once it gets there? Fortunately, his sperm were too stoned to do the job. And he was too stoned to keep a job. And, yes, I thought a solution to the problem was to buy a car and a laptop for a junkie. I was also a couple of steps away from buying a house in Jamaica with inheritance money so we could open up a bed-and-breakfast together. Because heroin, alcohol, and entrepreneurship go together so well.

The relationship conveniently kept me distracted from myself during the rare good moments and the more frequent bad ones. Unwilling to look at myself, I looked only at him—and blamed him for everything. I could find a way to make famine his fault. Clearly, I was crazy, too, though I couldn't see it.

Eventually, after enough disappointment, I could no longer avoid taking a real look at myself and my behavior. A friend told me, "If you find yourself obsessing, saying the same thing over and over about someone else, substitute your name for his and see if it still makes sense." So I tried it. Instead of saying, "He is such a liar; he keeps saying he'll quit and he never does," I substituted all the *he*'s with *I*'s. "*I* can't handle any life events without using. *I* care more about drinking than *I* do about him. *I* can't see how my drinking is related to the state of my life. *I* am a liar. *I* am an addict." *Fuck,* I realized, *I am an alcoholic.*

Prior to this exercise, I had concerns. I went to my mother on more than one occasion and said, "Mom, I am getting worried about my drinking." "Mom, I keep drinking and driving, and I am scaring myself." To which she would simply reply, "Don't worry, you'll grow out of it." That was not what I wanted to hear.

I wanted her to care. To try and stop me. To panic and worry and express concern. I wanted an intervention. I wanted her to say, *Enough is enough—I will not stand for this anymore.* But it wasn't happening. Like a toddler, I kept engaging in dangerous activities, hoping my mommy would step in and create boundaries to keep me safe.

But my poor mother was not raised for that job. She grew up on a bar stool next to her old man. She grew up mixing booze and 7UP for her father while he was driving. She had a liquor-hiding, in-and-out-of-hospitals, dead-on-a-barroom-floor-at-forty-nine kind of dad. She was not trained to set boundaries. She was trained to enable. I had to reach a moment when I decided to care for myself regardless of what anyone else was going to do.

When the pipe dream of moving to Jamaica with my boyfriend fell through and it was clear that I would not be opening a bed-and-breakfast with an addict, I had to make some decisions. I had already quit my job, sublet my apartment, and sold all my belongings, fueled by delusions of palm trees and frozen drinks. Instead, I ended up moving into a rental property that my father owned in my hometown in upstate New York, two doors down from where he lived. The ex wasn't around to blame anymore, but my problems were not going away. My father asked me for $150 a month in rent, and I managed to pay it only twice. The other months I didn't have it to give him. I made a little money working part-time as a receptionist in a real estate office, and what I did make, I drank. It was a new job, and I had already called in sick twice and was gearing up to do it again.

A high school friend, Rachel, was visiting from L.A. Years before, we had shared an apartment on the Lower East Side and on one occasion had smoked so much pot that we did not just think we knew each other in a past life, we thought we were the same person. We would come home before dawn and wake the neighbors with impromptu bad-bongo-playing sessions or by blasting Prince for a full-on two-person dance party before we passed out. Needless to say, we were not permitted to resign the lease.

We decided to go for a walk together—a five-mile trail we had traveled many times growing up. For the entire walk, I confessed to her how I had grown fearful of my drinking. Fearful of how once I started, I was incapable of stopping. Now that the ex-boyfriend was out of the picture, I had no one to blame but myself. Despite my repeated attempts to go out and just have one, I'd find myself staying until the bitter end, until I was ejected by the bartender. How many more times was I going to go out with the intent of having a glass of wine only to hear the words "You don't have to go home, but you can't stay here"?

She listened. She empathized. She expressed concern. When we finished up the walk and were approaching our cars, she said, "I know this is fucked up, but I feel like having a glass of wine."

"Let's go," I said.

"Are you sure?" she asked.

"Yeah—it's not like I am going to quit today. Let's go."

"Okay, but we are just going to have one. We don't want to ruin ourselves for the party tomorrow night."

We had two. Or maybe three. She drove me home. But it had already started—the call of addiction, the burning in my chest that pulled me like a magnet to the next drink and would stop for nothing. It was impossible to ignore. As soon as she pulled out of the driveway, I was going out again. There was no doubt about it.

I woke up the next morning deathly hungover, coated in depression, debilitated by self-loathing, and said the word I had longed to hear from someone who cared. *Enough.*

Six and a half years later, a lot has changed. In sobriety, instead of running, I do what I can to sit still. I own a house and pay my mortgage every month. I have started my own business, and for the first time I do what I love for a living. I have adopted a dog and have a girlfriend. At thirty-eight, I consider my relationship with Julie the first one I have ever really been in.

When Julie asked me out, I tried to revert to my old ways. Even in sobriety, I was still more comfortable with the unavailable. Julie was beyond available. She liked me and let me know it, and it freaked me out. At the time, I was involved with someone who had just been let out of jail for vehicular manslaughter. After six months in recovery, he relapsed. On his first day out of rehab, he got behind the wheel and killed a woman walking down the street. He spent two years in jail, and when he was released, I started dating him. Four years into sobriety, and my taste was the same: inappropriate and unavailable.

So when Julie invited me on a date, I told her, "Sorry, it's just not the right time." She had a job and a degree, a car and a license. I'd never dated anyone like that. I was not that kind of girl.

But she was too good to pass up, so I went against my dysfunctional intuition and forced myself to give it a try. The first year and a half I spent in a full-on extended anxiety attack, constantly fighting the urge to break up with her. She was so into me. And the more she expressed her interest, the more I wanted to flee. I had to create rules to manage my panic—she was allowed to tell me I was pretty only three times a day, max. More than a few *I love you*'s, and I had heart palpitations.

It dawned on me that I was still running. Thankfully, a voice in my head told me to sit still and accept what I was being offered. Bear the discomfort, and the comfort will come. Julie and I are approaching our second year together, and she'll be moving in next month.

PART 3 CULTURE

FROM BAILEYS TO MANISCHEWITZ

"You can't be a real country unless you have a beer . . . it helps
if you have some kind of football team, or some nuclear
weapons, but at the very least you need a beer."
—Frank Zappa

LADIES AND GENTLEMEN, THE FABULOUS SLUR GIRLS

LAURIE LINDEEN

I WAS CRAWLING ON MY hands and knees on a filthy concrete dressing room floor in Tijuana, Mexico. This was not a scene from *Papillon*; this was me after a gig. It was 1993. My band, Zuzu's Petals, had just completed the most embarrassing blind-drunk set of our careers, and I was worried. Not so much worried because I was so intoxicated that I needed to puke. No. I was more fearful that we'd be kicked off our fabulous one-month, high-profile tour—opening for the dreamy new-wave swashbuckler Adam Ant—because I was behaving so unprofessionally. Zuzu's Petals' stock was finally rising, thanks to our well-received first album. With more people in the crowd, I felt more responsibility to put on a decent show and not be shitfaced.

Broken glass embedded itself in my palms and kneecaps as I dragged myself to the toilet, which sat bare and open in the dressing room. The toilet was made of cold metal, and it felt good on my forearms as I prepared myself to retch.

After I'd heaved a day's worth of tequila shots from Señor Toad's out of my system, I attempted to steady myself on my feet by leaning against a cinder-block wall. My forehead was sweaty, and there was a fresh tear around the armhole of my lacy, off-white vintage first-communion dress. The pink satin bow marking the center of my Peter Pan collar was untied.

Adam Ant's soundman and drum tech patted me on the back and said, "You girls are our heroes." There is no privacy on the rock 'n' roll road. People puke, fornicate, and practice all other manners of self-relief in public if there's no alternative.

We had been perhaps a little too well behaved, too demure and careful in the eyes of the veteran crew. Now that we'd attempted to perform blind drunk, followed by a public puking session, we were welcomed members of the club—we were bona fide rockers.

Musicians, like house painters, writers, and actors, are often presumed drinkers. I like to blame as much as I possibly can on Frank Sinatra—a tough enigma to crack. He embodied that near-impossible alchemy of even parts stone-cold talent, charisma, tenacity, and a soft heart with a jigger of total douche-baggery sprinkled in for complexity. The Sinatra-led Rat Pack made being hammered onstage look like so much fun, like such a laugh riot. Look at Frank, Sammy, and Dean, all so loose, sexy, and cool—highball in one hand, smoke in the other. Everybody wanted them. Nobody loved it very much when Shirley MacLaine filled in for the ailing Dean Martin. That swinging men's club image was so seductive that even well into the 1980s, many of us subconsciously clung to that model. Who wouldn't want to be fun and funny while smoking, drinking, and singing? What could be better? Nothing.

In creating Zuzu's Petals, an all-women band, there was a presumed strength in numbers. We were sisters in our cups. After our tipsy performances, fans would congratulate us, saying things like, "You guys really rock, for girls!" and, "You girls look like you're having a lot of fun up there!" while offering to buy us shots. But they weren't clawing to get to us—they wanted to service the band dudes, no matter how wasted and skanky they were. Sad but true.

Back in my rock band days, there were a host of terrific drinking buddies in our constellation of Minneapolis-based male musician friends: the Replacements, Soul Asylum, the Jayhawks. We also made plenty of new male drinking pals on the road: Best Kissers in the World, Otis Coyote, the Fuzztones. We could hold our own with any of them. It was the late eighties and early nineties—everyone drank because everyone's parents drank. We drank because it was fun and it was how otherwise socially challenged artistic types could comfortably socialize.

And then there were the female booze-loving musicians—our role models. Like Janis Joplin, Chrissie Hynde, Joni Mitchell, Deborah Harry, Peggy Lee, and the Go-Gos (all above average in the cool category). We, too, enjoyed the grape, along with our contemporary female musicians: Kim Deal of the Pixies, half of L7, Babes in Toyland (original trio), Shawn Colvin, Lucinda Williams, and two-thirds of the band Scrawl, to name a few. Cool women in the arts drank, like Zelda Fitzgerald and Greta Garbo ("Give me a whiskey, baby . . . and don't be stingy").

It was all fun and games until somebody lost a life. Bob Stinson of the Replacements was the first close-to-home casualty, and it was drugs, not drink, that finally did him in. But there is no hierarchy in substance abuse or a preferred way to go; gone is gone. A lot of us who drank also dabbled in drugs, and some folks got hooked.

The women of Zuzu's Petals just wanted to have fun. We'd just pulled in for a sound check at First Avenue, a nightclub in downtown Minneapolis where Zuzu's Petals paid endless dues. We'd clawed our way into the main room, the big concert venue with the proper stage and sound system—the best stage in town.

The crew of stage managers and sound people began to refer to us as the Slur Girls—we had a reputation for slurring our words after too much drink. They even named a cocktail after us, a tall, red, delicious drink made with Absolut Kurant, cranberry juice, and lemon. "It's the Slur Girls!" they'd say when they saw us tearing around the club all night in various stages of uproarious laughter, clutching our cocktails and vintage handbags.

Drinking went out of vogue for a stretch in the early 1990s with the advent of straight-edge punk and the riot grrrls, a postfeminist, female-centric musical movement with strong political leanings. Some of them were vegans in favor of abstinence. Some turned to heroin. Neither group talked to us much when we played together on the road. We Slur Girls were fine with that; we were busy not taking ourselves too seriously. When once asked by a music journalist if we considered ourselves riot grrrls, my bandmate Co purred, "We're not riot grrrls. We're a riot." Already veterans of the road and the recording industry by the time the riot grrrls came out growling, we had worked hard to avoid being pigeonholed. Nevertheless, we would forever be labeled a chick band.

Back in the so-called day, I had horrendous stage fright, and a couple of drinks did wonders. Today I find myself on that same First Avenue stage once a year, thanks to a charitable friend who asks me to dust myself off and sing a David Bowie song to help raise money for a no-kill cat shelter. I love this event, Rock for Pussy (or Bowie Night, as I call it around my son). Local musicians, old and new, perform an evening of all Bowie songs. My excited anticipation of this evening borders on manic.

As it did when I was a Slur Girl, the old model still grabs hold of me—a few drinks, but not too many, before going on. Too many cocktails, and you get "drunk voice," that terrible audience-punishing phenomenon where your voice gets stuck in a two-note range but you think you sound like dynamite. Drunk voice is embarrassing.

One year at Rock for Pussy, I was granted the crown prince of Bowie songs, "Rock 'n' Roll Suicide." I had too many drinks while catching up with old friends backstage, and then it was my turn to hit the stage. Clad in a purple-and-black corset, with fresh lilac sprigs in my hair, I reconnected with my inner Slur Girl, the alcohol allowing me to forget for a few moments that I'm now Middle-Aged Woman with Endless Responsibilities. "Time takes a cigarette . . . " I rasped.

My crappy performance is still up there online somewhere, I'm told, and it makes me cringe. I croaked and overemoted like Norma Desmond. My voice sucked because I had drunk too much. The image of the drunken presuicidal Anne Sexton performing her poetry with young hipster musician/fans in Cambridge, Massachusetts, haunts me. It's at the top of my situations-to-avoid list.

Last year at Rock for Pussy, I was assigned Bowie's "Queen Bitch." To prepare, I sang quietly to myself a cappella while walking my dog. I no longer allow myself more than two beers before my turn on Bowie Night and never a Slur Girl cocktail, nerves or no nerves.

Almost twenty years after the fact, I have to ask myself: Did I create a band and forge a career in music because it was a job at which one is pretty much expected to drink? As with all tricky questions, the answer is not cut-and-dried.

Rock shows, parties, dancing, singing, hanging with friends, book clubs, luncheons, great conversations, gatherings of all types, and travel are among my favorite things to do in the world. All those activities are exceptionally drinker-friendly, and that's when I like to drink. I'm naturally very social.

When I shut in or isolate myself, however, I tend to fall into the abyss of depression. I never drink alone. I keep a dry house. I am, in middle age, mindful not to overdrink, mostly because hangovers become increasingly brutal with age, and I can't afford to miss a day, but also because drunk, oldish women are viewed unfavorably. Drunken male musician onstage? No big deal. Funny. Caddish. Charming. Drunken chick onstage? Pathetic. Sad. Out of control. So many things are still not fair.

I recently emailed my former bandmates, asking them how they felt about our old moniker the Slur Girls. Our bassist's response was perfect: "In the '80s it was kind of a badge of honor. Today, not so much."

MAN-O-MANISCHEWITZ!

DAPHNE MERKIN

I CAN STILL REMEMBER with resounding clarity all these years later the note of horror in my mother's voice the first time she called me and I sounded audibly drunk. I must have been in my early twenties. I was living in a dark little apartment all the way over on the less genteel reaches of the Upper East Side and had come home after an evening in which much alcohol had been imbibed. I was delighting in the feeling that being drunk gave me—that floaty, nothing-can-get-at-you sensation of being freed from the usual confines of your mind. I was happy being drunk, and I suppose this, as much as the fact that I was slurring my words, is what took my mother so aback.

"You sound drunk," she said, in a tone heavy with accusation.

"Really?" I said. "I think I am."

There was silence for a moment, reverberating across the wire like a scream.

"Daphne," she said. "Jews don't drink."

It was a statement, not an implicit question, a categorical imperative born of ethnic pride and a hierarchical sense of differentiation: *Jews don't drink*. It was something other people did—goyim, to be exact—to their detriment. It was something people like us didn't do, to our betterment. True, there was the holiday of Purim, the one time during the year when Jews were encouraged to drink to the point of muddledness—until they could no longer distinguish between the heroes and the villains in the Purim story, between the phrases *"arur Haman"* (cursed is Haman) and *"baruch* Mordechai" (blessed is Mordechai). But this was a singular exception in a largely teetotaling religion. To drink was to fall out of Jewishness into a sea of unruly impulses and ungovernable behavior. Who knew what I might take up next?

I GREW UP IN A RELIGIOUSLY observant home, one where the laws of kashruth and Shabbos were rigorously adhered to and cocktails were a thing unheard of. We ate something called Smokey Bear cookies instead of Oreos, for instance, because Nabisco didn't specify vegetable oil in its ingredients, so there was a chance Oreos contained animal fat. In the twenty-four-hour period from Friday night to Saturday night, when Shabbos ended, we didn't use electricity—no phones, no lights, no TV or music. Friday night was the one night the family in its entirety—my parents and the six of us kids— sat down to eat together; the rest of the week my parents ate on their own in the dining room while my siblings and I had dinner in the kitchen. It was an odd, slightly *Upstairs Downstairs* arrangement, true to the Victorian coloration of our family life, but it highlighted the totemic significance of those Friday night dinners.

The table was always beautifully set—my mother was stronger on aesthetics than on providing a feeling of familial warmth—with a linen tablecloth and napkins, flowers, good china, and stemware; the last included matching water and wine glasses. The chandelier glistened, the sterling silver cutlery and candlesticks gleamed, and the very atmosphere seemed to shimmer with anticipation.

The kiddush benediction my father made before the meal called for the first introduction of booze into our weekly menu. This took the form of a bottle of Manischewitz when I was very young, although in later years, when the manufacture of kosher wines came into its own, we moved on to the more sophisticated Israeli label of Carmel, which in turn was succeeded by other labels such as Yarden and Kedem.

"Man-o-Manischewitz! What a wine!" That's how the punch line of the TV and radio commercials for this generic wine went, blunt as could be. I liked everything about Manischewitz's Concord grape wine, from its deep burgundy color to its cloyingly sweet taste—a heightened, fermented form of grape juice. I liked that you didn't have to get used to it the way you had to work your way into a fondness for other adult libations, from scotch to coffee. Its taste was immediately appealing, whether served up in little white paper cups at a synagogue kiddush after morning services on Saturday or in a large silver goblet that was passed around for everyone to take a sip from at the dinner table. I even liked the definitive stains it used to leave on everything, from the table-cloth to my best Shabbos dresses, letting you know of its presence.

Jewish laws around wine and wine making are complex, having been refined and codified over centuries by the rabbinate to ensure maximal sanctity for this beverage. The regulations governing ko-sher wine basically stem from a fear of drinking, leading to a letting down of the guard between Jews and non-Jews (and from there lead-ing to a breaking of the taboo against intermarriage).

Accordingly, my family's non-Jewish help weren't allowed to handle the wine bottles; these were always taken out of the fridge and placed on the table inside a silver container by my mother. (The exception to this rule is wine that is boiled, called *yayin mevush-al,* which can be served by non-Jews.) I eventually moved on from Manischewitz and developed an affection for the lighter white wines served on Friday night and again at Shabbos lunch. I don't remem-ber there ever being more than two bottles opened at a single meal, which suggests very restrained amounts were imbibed, since we were a large family and several guests were usually in attendance as well.

WINE WAS FEATURED AT meals a few other times of the year, mostly on Jewish holidays major and minor, ranging from Rosh Ha-shanah to Shavuos. The Passover seder called for drinking four full cups of wine over its duration, but I remember many of our guests opting for grape juice after the first two cups, fearful of the stupefying effects too much wine would have on them. There was one regular seder guest, my mother's close friend Hilde, who would barrel her way through the four cups of wine with great application; she would invariably end up a bit tipsy by the seder's end, much to my mother's visible annoyance. Indeed, I think of Hilde to this day as one of the few robust drinkers among my parents' acquaintances, but I'm sure she appears to me in this light only by contrast with the feeble level of inebriation around her.

There was one dessert on my mother's very repetitive Shabbos menus (written down by her on white notepads every week for our cook, the faithful Iva, to put into effect) that was memorable for me in part because it called for a splash of alcohol. It was a very good nondairy chocolate mousse, made with egg whites rather than heavy cream, and the liquid in question was schnapps.

The only other exceptions to Shabbos and holiday wine were the discreet bottles of liquor housed in a small wine cabinet built into one of the bookcases that lined my father's study. This cabinet lit up when you opened it, to my childish delight. It usually contained one or two gift-wrapped bottles of wine cordial or Chivas Regal brought by grateful dinner guests, as well as a bottle or two of the plum brandy known as slivovitz and the occasional bottle of whiskey or port. When my Belgian grandmother came for visits from Israel, the collection expanded to include a bottle or two of Bols, the bright yellow eggnog drink she favored.

I suffered from insomnia as a young girl. Sometimes when I couldn't fall asleep at night, my mother poured me a shot glass of slivovitz. I loved standing with her in the darkened study with just the illumination from the cabinet, having her all to myself, dawdling over my drink to delay going back to bed for as long as possible. This was my first—and only—exposure to the consolations of alcohol, but being the fairly compliant creature I was, it never occurred to me when I became older to nip at the port, much less break into the liquor cabinet and have a serious go at its contents.

Then again, for the longest time, possibly because it was neither entirely prohibited nor explicitly embraced, the mind-altering potential of hard drinking didn't entice me. This was in direct contrast with what I witnessed taking place during my daughter's high school years, when all the parents at her private girls' school were up in arms lest a drop of alcohol be consumed at any social gathering. This zealously phobic attitude toward the dangers of drinking could only, I surmised, be the product of parental backgrounds where an alcoholic relative or two lurked in every corner. At the Jewish day school I attended throughout the sixties and early seventies, I remember discussions about sex and drugs, but I don't recall the perils of drinking ever coming up as a subject to be contended with.

MY FIRST SERIOUS encounter with the phenomenon known as cocktail hour came through literature rather than life, via the writings of O'Hara, Updike, and Cheever. Their depictions of WASP suburban angst wouldn't be complete without the clink of ice cubes and the burbling of alcohol being poured in the background. It was through reading that I discovered the crucial, even sacrosanct place the rituals of drinking held in the American imagination—the ingenious way alcohol seemed to lubricate everything from onerous chitchat to self-conscious sexual advances. I also came to realize the tragic grip the "sorrows of gin," to borrow the title from a Cheever story, exerted on those who succumbed to its baleful influence. I was sufficiently intrigued by the special lure it held for writers to seek out a book called *The Thirsty Muse*, about the destructive effect alcohol had on four American writers.

This familiarity remained largely theoretical until my twenties, when I became friendly for the first time with people who actually observed cocktail hour in its full regalia. These included my friend

Elizabeth Harper, whose parents were assimilated Jews to such an extent that Elizabeth herself hadn't been aware she was Jewish until high school. I would go to her parents' spare modernist house in Rye for the weekend and be riveted when the afternoon drew close to the five thirty hour, when arrangements for predinner drinks would begin. These included the setting out of cheese and peanuts in the living room and the much-deliberated-over selection of a piece of classical music.

We would gather, just the four of us, with drinks in hand—generally wine, as I recall—and settle in for a painstakingly impersonal conversation about some suitably cultural topic, be it books or art or the latest theater. I felt incredibly adult in a way I never felt in my parents' home, but at the same time there was something discordant about the intimacy of the setting and the mellowing effect of the wine as it played out against the formalized tenor of our interaction. Here I had associated alcohol with forays into sloshy emotions and unwarranted confessions; indeed, I had thought that was partly its purpose, to unleash the previously confined id into a room of no-longer-watchful superegos. Having drinks with Elizabeth and her parents made me realize that you could enter the convivial realm of social drinking and still remain tight as a clam inside, that alcohol loosened you up only if you gave it your tacit permission to do so.

I would go on to be present at many more cocktail hours over the next three decades, and I learned that in the world outside Orthodox Judaism, Jews drank with gusto. I discovered that my own tolerance for alcohol—notwithstanding my mother's cautionary remarks about the natural nonfit between Jews and drinking—was pretty high. There were a couple of years when I worked in publishing during the late eighties and early nineties when I regularly downed two or three Bloody Marys before lunch was served, but I don't remember ever feeling more than a tiny bit overrun; certainly I never had any problem going back to the office after lunch and continuing where I had left off.

I eventually counted two bona fide alcoholics among my friends—one an Irish woman writer who thought nothing of gulping down a glass of whiskey with her breakfast, and the other a radio personality who required that I stock his preferred brand of scotch for when he came over. Nowadays there is a staggering variety of kosher wines, both domestic and imported, to choose from. And although it's not something I'd readily admit to the wine snobs I know, the truth is that despite my more contemporary affinity for rieslings from Alsace and sancerres from the Loire Valley, I have never lost my love for Manischewitz from Newark, New Jersey. Unrefined and oft ridiculed, it's still the softest hard drink I know, redolent with memory and pure grapey pleasure.

VENI, VIDI, BIBI (I CAME, I SAW, I DRANK)

HELENE STAPINSKI

I LOVE TO DRINK. Most people assume this comes from my mother's pleasure-seeking Italian side. But in truth, the Italians in my family are not real drinkers, enjoying only the occasional glass of wine. I get my drinking love and stamina from my Polish father. Through the years, I've gone shot for shot with dog mushers in Alaska over Yukon Jack. I outdrank my husband with a bottle of Mekong whiskey on a beach in Thailand. I even kept up with a group of Russians, who taught me the right way to drink vodka.

Not long ago, however, on a mission to research a family mystery, I learned that alcohol runs deep, very deep, in my Italian heritage. I went to a restaurant in Manhattan called Pisticci, named after the small hilltop village in southern Italy where my great-great-grandmother lived a century ago. When I met the restaurant owner, Michael, and Rosalba, a woman visiting from the actual town of Pisticci (pronounced *Pist-EECH),* they were excited to hear about my upcoming trip, since hardly anyone ever visits Pisticci. The real Pisticci.

"What's your family name?" asked Rosalba.

"Vena," I said.

"Oh my God! Have you tried Amaro Lucano?!"

I had never even heard of Amaro Lucano. From her bag, she pulled out a tall bottle of brown liquor, which she'd carried nearly five thousand miles to deliver to Michael. "This is the local *digestivo* from Pisticci. It is made by the Vena family!" She looked at me, exclamation points flying out of her eyes.

I looked at the unfamiliar yellow label, featuring our family name, Vena, and a woman dressed in the traditional Italian blousy costume—a classic figure called the *pacchiana*. Her hair is pulled up off her neck, and her hand is on her hip in a saucy pose. She's looking off the edge of the bottle, probably at some poor old Italian guy out of frame. *What are you,* stunad? you can hear her say. She's smirking. I'm known in my family for my smirk, much like the Mona Lisa's (who's from the same region, incidentally).

With her other hand, this long-lost animated *paesana* is holding a basket of herbs, representing what's inside the bottle. No one actually knows what's inside, however, since it's a Vena family secret—like Colonel Sanders's eleven secret herbs and spices.

"You must try some!" Rosalba exclaimed. Michael grabbed a glass and poured, the liquid viscous and thick. I licked my lips.

But this. This was different. The Amaro Lucano packed a hidden, special punch, one that would not make itself known for months, like some lingering cosmic hangover that takes a while to kick in.

For starters, it smelled like Jägermeister. And I hate Jägermeister. My nostrils flared, but I quickly shot it back and tried not to grimace, for fear I would insult Michael and Rosalba. Suddenly I was transported back to age seven, lying on the couch with fever and a bad cough, being forced to swallow the nastiness on the spoon. This did not taste like Jäger. It tasted like Vicks Formula 44.

"What do you think?" Rosalba asked.

"Delicioso!" I lied.

"Would you like another?" Michael graciously offered. I must've lied too enthusiastically.

"Oh, no, thank you. I get drunk very easily," I lied again. To distract them from pouring more, I told them my story, the fractured, complicated story that was sending me on a trip to southern Italy that summer—my Vena family mystery.

At the turn of the last century, Vita, my great-great-grandmother, murdered someone in southern Italy during a card game. She fled to America with her three sons but left her husband, Francesco Vena, behind. He followed thirty years later.

On her way to America, Vita lost one of her sons. We don't know how or where. Whether he fell overboard in Naples or ran away. We don't even know his name. All we know is that Vita escaped to Jersey City in 1892 with the teenage Valentin and Leonardo, my great-grandfather.

Relatives always said that Val and Leonardo had different fathers and that our real last name was Greco. Leonardo's wife used to call Vita, her mother-in-law, *puttanella*—little whore. They didn't get along. But then again, hardly anyone did on the Italian side of the family.

We didn't know much about the murder—not the victim's name or the murder weapon. My mother never got the whole story because Vita died in 1915 after being hit in the head with a sock full of rocks on Mischief Night, long before my mother was born. My family considered it karmic revenge for Vita's crime. *"Chi la fa, l'aspetti!"* they'd say. What goes around comes around. When Vita's husband, Francesco, came to America and found out that Vita was dead, he turned around and went back to Pisticci.

Soon after the evening I first tasted Amaro Lucano, I made my own overseas voyage to dig up Vita's story. I brought along my mother, my two small children, and my friend-turned-translator, Tony, whose family hailed from nearby Calabria.

We stayed on the arch of Italy's boot, in the town of Bernalda—the same town that spawned Francis Ford Coppola's family. I'd rented an apartment for one month on the street where Vita grew up, Via Cavour, and sealed the deal with my landlady over a shot of *limoncello*. If only the Vena family made *limoncello*.

Every morning I woke to the sound of either the fish man yelling, *"Pesce!"* through a megaphone or my neighbor screaming at her sons across the way—without a megaphone. I'm not sure who was louder.

I'd also be spending a lot of time in Pisticci, the neighboring village, where Vita had lived before leaving for America. After about three minutes in Pisticci, I spotted Bar Vena, a small café on Piazza Umberto. Tony and I ran inside to see if they knew anything about Vita's mysterious crime.

When I told the bartender my story and my family name, he turned and quickly pulled down a bottle of—you guessed it—Amaro Lucano. Before I could stop him, he placed a glass on the polished bar and poured me a shot. He nodded at Tony, asking if he wanted one. *"No grazie,"* Tony said, waving him off. If I refused this drink, I'd insult the bartender and he wouldn't tell me a thing. I gritted my teeth, lifted the glass, and forced a smile.

After much back-and-forth in barely intelligible dialect, it turned out he knew nothing of the Vita story. I turned to Tony, hand on my saucy hip, and complained in English, "I drank that whole friggin' shot for nothing."

Next I went to meet a man named Evaristo, a local policeman married to a relative of Rosalba, the woman I'd met at the Manhattan restaurant. After driving around for about ten minutes, I parked and greeted Evaristo as if I'd known him for thirty years, then introduced him to Tony. They hugged.

"Humido," said Evaristo, fanning himself with one hand. A Roman, transplanted here to Pisticci, Evaristo led us quickly through the streets to a neighborhood that looked terribly familiar. And there, in front of us, was Bar Vena—the place we'd just been—"founded by the same family that makes Amaro Lucano," Evaristo explained. I told him we'd just been there. Once inside, he pointed to a shelf way above the bar containing a horrifyingly large bottle of Amaro Lucano.

"Would you like a shot?" Evaristo asked.

I vigorously shook my head no. For the next several weeks, I was offered glass after glass of Amaro Lucano every time I mentioned my family name. It became my penance for seeking the family's original sin.

After a quick espresso, Evaristo took us to the municipal building, where we searched for my great-great-grandparents' marriage certificate. No luck. We then visited the local church to search through crumbling yellowed papers, but there was no record there, either.

The next day we hit the streets and heard three different Vena murder stories from three different people: one about a man who shot a beggar through his door with a shotgun, one about a couple who killed a cuckolded husband with a scythe, and another that occurred in the 1950s. None of these murders was mine.

We then returned to the street where Vita had lived before her escape—where her son, my great-grandfather Leonardo, was born in 1879. Via Loreto. Below the street sign was a description of the neighborhood in English for tourists lost enough to have stumbled upon Pisticci:

> *This is the highest district. The site of the Medieval town, the only one which survived the 1688 landslide.... In this district there were: the homes of the Mayors, who were armed by the local squire, the houses of the priests, of the lawyers, of the doctors and the palatial residences which belonged to the noblest and wealthiest 17th and 18th century families.*

I WONDERED WHAT the hell Vita had been doing living in this swanky neighborhood. According to Leonardo's birth certificate, she was a weaver, and her husband, Francesco, a lowly farmer.

We found number 34, Vita's last address in Italy. The house was tiny and all white, except for its green shutters and door. The only sign of life, past or present, was an old clothesline stretched out front with a lone wooden clothespin, as if someone had left in a hurry and forgotten that last tiny belonging.

Evaristo canvassed the neighborhood and found out that no one had lived in Vita's old house for years. And no one seemed to know about the murder. They shrugged and recommended I speak to the town historian, Dino D'Angella.

We walked to the school where D'Angella worked as principal—also called *il presidente*. Evaristo led us to the main office, where we were intercepted by a squat woman with thick eyebrows and short dark hair.

Evaristo chatted heatedly with her. The woman shook her head and furrowed her impossibly bushy unibrow, then launched into a soliloquy.

"What's she saying?" I asked Tony.

"I don't know," he said, straining to keep up. "Maybe she's asking Evaristo if he has a pair of tweezers so she can pluck her eyebrows."

We were finally ushered into *il presidente*'s office. D'Angella was tall but stooped over. He had a balding pate of dark hair, a shining high forehead, very heavy lids over deep-set eyes, and a five o'clock shadow. He wore a thick gold chain attached to a gold Jesus head. His mouth was twisted in that familiar Basilicatan smirk.

"What can I do for you?" D'Angella asked.

"I'm an American writer researching my family history," I said. "It seems there was a murder involving my great-great-grandmother, who was from Bernalda, and her husband, who was from Pisticci."

"When did it happen?" he asked.

"Just over a hundred years ago. But no one I ask has ever heard of the murder."

He nodded, still smirking.

"What's the family name?" he asked.

"Vena."

"Well," he said. "My grandfather was a pharmacist." For a moment I feared he'd reach into his desk and pull out a large medicinal bottle of Amaro Lucano. But he simply paused for effect. "He knew all the village stories. And he had a good memory. He died in 1963, but for many years he would talk to me about famous crimes."

I nodded and moved to the edge of my chair.

"I remember a story he once told," D'Angella continued. "It had to do with one Francesco Vena."

All was still. "Around 1890 or so, this Francesco Vena killed someone."

Another long pause.

"Francesco Vena was tried and went to jail for about thirty years," D'Angella said, unaware of the gravity of his words. Thirty years. That's how long my great-great-grandfather Francesco had waited to come to America!

"My grandfather," he continued, "told me the murder had to do with a Gallitelli woman from Bernalda." Gallitelli was Vita's maiden name! Now exclamation points shot out of my eyes.

"Vita?!" I asked.

"I don't know the name Vita," he said, waving his hand. "Only Gallitelli. The way I heard it, she was not Francesco's wife. Not his lover either. They were simply living together."

This prison piece of the story explained why Francesco had stayed behind. Why it took him so long to follow the family over. And most important, why no one knew my story. I'd been telling it as if Vita had committed the crime. Which she probably had, according to my family lore. But Francesco had taken the rap.

I wanted to hug this angel from Pisticci, and he knew it. He sat there no longer with a smirk but with a self-satisfied grin.

Back in Bernalda, I tracked down two historians: Angelo Tataranno, a chain-smoking local *professore,* and Antonio Salfi. At a local café, we discussed my family history. I looked around at the other tables and noticed that I was the only woman among dozens of men. Women were home hanging laundry or buying fish. When I told them about Vita's, or Francesco's, homicidal card game, they nodded and said that many local murders were committed years ago over a popular card game called *passatella*. It wasn't just a card game but a drinking game as well.

Passatella, an ancient Roman invention, involved four principal players, though you could have as many as you liked. The more, the merrier. Or the more, the deadlier.

The winner of a round would be called king of the *passatella* and would get to hold the wine bottle, filling glasses for some and withholding wine from others. The king would then go around the table and explain why he was giving wine to some and not to the others, using insults and jokes, usually veiled in long speeches.

"But it would be very unusual for a woman to play *passatella*, or any card game," Tataranno said, taking a sip of *cedrata*, a bright green fluorescent drink that looks like antifreeze. (He offered me a shot of Amaro Lucano, but this time I declined.)

"Maybe Francesco had been playing and was insulted," I theorized, "and Vita took revenge later. Or maybe a fight broke out that night and the women ran to stop their husbands from killing each other, and one thing led to another . . . "

They collectively stuck out their bottom lip and gave it some thought. We started talking about research and how tricky it is, how luck has to be on your side. "I knew a man who did research under the wrong name for thirty years," lamented Tataranno. "His last name wasn't his last name at all. It's a tragic story, not knowing your last name."

"It's funny you say that," I said. "Because last night my mother and I were talking about how my grandfather always told her our name was not Vena at all, but Greco."

"That's interesting," said Salfi, "because Greco was the name of the wealthy landowners in Pisticci." He explained that the Grecos took concubines and treated their workers like slaves. They had extramarital affairs and children with the women. In some extreme cases, a rich man would ask a worker to marry his mistress or live with her.

"That way the woman would be taken care of day to day, but the rich man could visit her anytime," he continued. "When the *padrone*, or boss, arrived, the 'husband' would have to leave. It was a matter of life and death for the workers."

And suddenly it clicked into place. Why one son was sired by Vena and another by Greco. Why my family always said they had two different fathers. And two different names. This is why Vita and Francesco had no marriage certificate, why it's not recorded in the church. The Pisticci connection. Moving to that house in the fancy part of town.

Vita was a kept woman, a concubine. A *puttanella,* like my great-grandmother always said. We are descendants of Greco the wealthy landowner and his concubine, Vita.

After two weeks of fruitlessly digging through criminal archives, we decided to visit the Amaro Lucano factory, just in case those Venas were related to my Venas. The town was lousy with Venas—more than thirty-five in the phone book. I'd avoided the factory all this time because perched on top of the building was a giant cardboard Amaro Lucano bottle on its side. It scared me; it was so big.

We parked in the company lot, which had a rusty yellow gate with blue letters that spelled out my family name. My fake family name, anyway: VENA.

We walked up to the guard building and explained that we were long-lost relatives and wanted to speak with the owners. The guard was friendly but said that the Venas were at a family reunion. At first I thought, *Damn. If only I had known, I could've gone along.* But then I realized I would have had to consume large quantities of Amaro Lucano. Better I didn't go.

He told us to return another time, but we were leaving the following day. "Do you have any information about the Vena family?" I asked. "A family tree?"

"No family tree," he said. "But there is something." He reached into his desk—for what I'm convinced was a complimentary bottle of Amaro Lucano—and came up with a hardcover book on the company history. I flipped through the pages, getting lost in the sepia-colored photos of Pisticci and the company founder, Pasquale, born in 1871, around the same time as Leonardo and Valentin. According to the book, Pasquale went to Naples with his brothers and watched them sail for America. But he stayed behind and got a job.

Three brothers. In Naples. Two sailing to America. All named Vena.

And it hit me.

Could his brothers have been Leonardo and Valentin? Could Pasquale have been that other child, lost along the way? Impossible. But what if it was the same family? I began to get dizzy with excitement. Here I was, dreading the bitter Amaro Lucano every time someone offered me a glass. Was my family link so obvious, right here on the label of the bottle? Maybe that was Vita, a cocky woman with a smirk, her hand on her hip as if to say, *Ehhhh. Waddayoudo? Not much of a detective!*

"Can I buy a copy?" I asked.

"You can have that one," said the guard.

"Thank you," I said, clutching it to my chest.

And with that—with the hope of a clue, a link, a much more happy ending—we left Pisticci.

Maybe Pasquale was Vita's son, who didn't drown or die at all but stayed behind in Naples, making a fresh cut from his murderess mother. In the coming months, I wrote letters and made calls to the Amaro Lucano company. But they ignored me, that crazy American woman writer.

On our last day in Italy, I packed our bags, leaving out the summer clothes that wouldn't fit the kids the following year. In their place, I packed three bottles of Amaro Lucano, my new favorite beverage.

A CHINESE AMERICAN GIRL: DRINKING FROM EAST TO WEST

EMMA KATE TSAI

I NEVER SAW MY FATHER with a drink in his hand; I never saw my mother without one. But my parents were never side by side when I saw them. I am a product of two extremes—half-Chinese, half-American. East and West met in my horribly mismatched parents, then melded in their three offspring: my brother, my sister, and me.

My parents separated when I was two, causing me to bounce between my father's modest suburban house, which I considered home, and my mother's dank apartment, which I considered beneath me. The crack in their relationship—I hesitate to call it a marriage, because most of it happened outside the bounds of matrimony—started to form early, much before my time. And it wasn't only the drink that came between my parents, but politics, upbringing, and a value system they didn't share. The world had drawn a line between them, and they finally submitted to its existence once and for all.

Born in China and raised in Taiwan, my father bore all the markings of a traditional Chinese man. He was diligent, loyal, faithful, steady, disciplined, responsible, and serious. And my mother? Well, she was American. She gave in easily and often to temptation, and that included drinking. Nevertheless, I loved them both.

Swinging back and forth between them, I sometimes emulated my father and sometimes my mother, as if each parent's persona were simply a mask to be worn at that particular moment. And when it came to drinking, I was just as confused. Would I be the lush my mother had always been or the teetotaler my father boasted of being?

I was more like my Chinese father but wanted to be more like my American mother. She was the exciting one, the pretty one, the fun one, the easy-to-be-with one. The one who drank. The single woman. She laughed; he yelled. And though I respected my father's choices, the model of my mother's lifestyle dangled like a glittering mobile I could never fully shut out of my mind. I began to associate drinking with playfulness, youth, and going out. And being American.

My mother's language was drinking. She spoke it and lived it, giving the drink more power in her home than she gave herself, a regular and higher placement at the lunch and dinner table and the role of main character in her every story. The drink, and my mother, brought men home, strange men we never saw again. But she didn't just *show* us what it was to be a drinker; she *taught* us. When I was twelve, she gave me a sip of her wine. I asked her once if I could try her beer, but I spit it out before I could swallow it. I remember one of her trademark lines: "No one drinks beer for the taste. It's just like coffee that way." My siblings and I had to play along, and we all did or she'd mark us as "your father's child"—something ugly, bad, and not her. Mom was happy when she drank, giggling until she cried in a way that I loved. But sometimes it made her sad.

My mother drank like the typical American male. When I heard the refrigerator door squeak open and then slam shut, I knew she was headed for the couch with a cold brew. Light beer was her beverage of choice. She drank it straight from the bottle—in front of the television, with lunch, as she cooked dinner, before she went out, on her way to bed. Koozies—those chintzy foam protectors—blanketed the top of our fridge, the bottom shelf of the pantry, the hall closet. They were like an infestation of alcoholism that we—or the apartment—could never be rid of. I had no idea they even had a name.

Shot glasses acted as our passport through Mom's travels around the world, keeping our cabinet doors from shutting and leaving little room for our sippy cups and water glasses. It was the only way we knew where she'd been when she left us—she was never around for very long. When she left town, she placed us in our father's care. She rarely sent postcards; she hardly ever called. But when she came home, we'd visit her in the next apartment she'd moved to, discovering a tiny new drinking glass with the latest state or country of her travels etched into its side.

Late at night, when I couldn't sleep, I'd sneak into the dark kitchen and fill one of her shot glasses with apple juice. I felt closer to my mother when I did—as if I had been there with her, as if I'd stood behind her as she'd bought each and every piece of alcoholic-drink ware. Then I'd stare at the Budweiser-magneted fridge and photos of my mother drinking a frozen cocktail through a brightly colored straw. More souvenirs lived in the freezer. Alongside the Popsicles and frozen peas lay frosted beer mugs that she'd slipped into her purse at taverns around town. Those were branded, too: BIG ASS BEER and the name of the bar, usually Woodrow's. It was the first time I'd seen the word *ass* in print. When I asked my mom what it meant, she laughed and pushed me away.

Of everything surrounding the way my mother drank, what thrilled me most were the stories of escapades that she joyfully retold around the coffee table. Every one of her nights out started with a killer ensemble and one of her discarded boyfriends recently demoted to the distinguished role of babysitter for the night. I could paint the image of my mother standing against a door: She was beautiful and scintillating, but not in a way that made sense for a mother to be. Black leggings, a low-cut black tank top, bright pink lipstick, dark blue eye shadow, long dangling earrings.

Drinking was more than just a kitchen collectible or a pastime that made her seem cooler than every typical aproned mother. She had horrible luck with cars. At least that's what I thought. When I got older, I learned why my mother kept getting in "accidents" and why my father, whom she'd long before divorced, kept buying her new modes of transportation. She cycled through her list of reasons for each wreck—hit-and-run; the car had been stolen; a friend had borrowed it. Eventually I realized that most of the time she'd fallen asleep at the wheel after a night of drinking.

I mouthed off to my mother early and often. But it wasn't until I spoke out against her drinking ("Mom, are your beers getting bigger?") that she sent me to my room. I refused to apologize, and eventually we silently agreed to pretend she wasn't drinking more and I wasn't noticing. In fact, her beers *were* getting bigger, as was she. Her weight gain came on fast and strong, and it embarrassed me. I used to wonder how different my life would've been if my parents had stayed married. Perhaps it would have been just the same.

I never saw my father drink. The only alcoholic beverage to ever take up space in his PG-rated home was wine he received as a gift, left corked on the sideboard in our dining room. I would look over at the bottle—before he'd regift it to an American colleague—in between bites of dinner at the plastic-covered dining table.

We spent holidays with my father, since Mom went notoriously missing on New Year's Eve and other traditional celebrations. The movies taught me about those festive evenings and how American families celebrated and drank. I learned about spiked punch, alcohol-laden eggnog, and cider mixed with brandy. All of us—the three kids, my father, and the Chinese friends he'd made his family—drew numbers after a potluck dinner for White Elephant, a game we played. Our throats stayed dry. No one drank. No one brought wine even; everyone brought food.

We toasted with food. Instead of beginning with an aperitif, we bit into an eggroll. Instead of popping open a bottle of champagne, we raised our bowls in celebration. And we always overdid it. Every meal commenced with a collection of appetizers, followed by up to ten dishes (*gai lan,* steamed bok choy, stir-fried green beans, ground pork and tofu, roasted duck, cold steamed chicken, a whole steamed fish, egg scrambled with tomatoes), followed by an imaginative soup (sometimes as simple as seaweed and water), and concluding with dessert (soup made with sweet red beans or egg custard) and fruit.

But it wasn't just the focus on food that kept our bellies empty of wine. It was being Chinese. I could feel it, even then: the focus on abstinence, the wariness of indulgent behavior. The risk was too great. It might mean a loss of control, and that could mean something much worse: a loss of self-respect. My father lived a life of integrity, and that meant not getting drunk. Abstaining from alcohol fit nicely with the rest of his and his friends' Chinese ideals—loyalty, fidelity, reverence, humility, respect. I respected him and his self-discipline. I didn't respect my mother.

Instead of the shot glasses that claimed premium shelf space in my mother's tiny kitchen, regular drinking glasses and plastic cups got prime real estate in my father's. The few wineglasses he did own—wedding gifts to him and his second wife (he remarried when I was eleven)—sat tucked away in the back, collecting dust.

I watched my father tell his stories, just as I watched my mother tell hers. I didn't understand a single word of the Mandarin he spoke, but I knew that his anecdotes didn't need the help of alcohol to spill out, as my mother's did. The bottles of Ozark spring water in his friends' hands clued me in. At those Chinese-only gatherings, there was never any alcohol in sight. I saw my father break this unspoken rule only on the rare occasions he invited Americans to the house, when he stocked ice chests with Budweiser along with cans of Coke and bottles of water. He made his prejudice very clear: Americans drank; Chinese didn't. But I took it as a cultural norm, one that confused me. I was a Chinese American. What kind of drinker would that make me?

I tried my first beer on my own when I was going on eighteen. A freshman in college, I'd made my first friend in biology class, a Mexican guy whose wallet was attached to his pants by a metal chain. He was like no one I'd ever met. I was the teacher's pet, the girl with glasses who sat in the back row making straight A's. I wasn't cool. But this guy was. His name was Francisco (Cisco), and he taught me that drinking was not only a rite of passage but a skill. I quickly learned the rules of the game.

I don't remember if he asked if I ever drank before; I think he just assumed that I had. I can't blame him, really. I was introverted and shy, and people often mistook that for experienced and coy. But I was neither, even when I so desperately wanted to be. I took my first voluntary drink in his dorm room in the middle of the day. It felt like truancy. He popped open a tiny refrigerator door and offered me a Guinness. I couldn't say no. I had to be cool. I was in college now. After I let the cold liquid burn my throat, I felt deflowered, as if it—and he—had taken a piece of my virginity. As if I had been raped of my sobriety. I'd wanted to say no, truly, but it was as if I'd be exiled from college life if I did.

But this—drinking—wasn't me. I felt like I was cheating on myself. I hated the feel of the bottle in my hand, the glass on my lip, the taste of it, the way it felt going down. I hated it for being a vice. For being my mother's vice. And in using it, I was letting down my father, the person whose very core character I knew I had within me. But drink I did, for altogether different reasons than my mother did. I didn't need it and didn't care if I ever drank again. I did it because drinking was being young and single and cute. And for a moment, that's what I wanted to be.

"You don't want to be social with those kinds of people," my father once said after seeing me with Cisco, the boy with dark skin and baggy jeans. His disapproval made me feel as if the beer had stained my teeth with paternal infidelity. Suddenly I remembered all that I loved about my mother—her twinkling eyes, her Marilyn Monroe mouth, her transcendent beauty, her charm, her likability. The alcohol made her that way, I convinced myself. It turned her volume up and made her the belle of the ball. The booze took away any self-consciousness that made her as hesitant as the rest of us were. And it was the drink that would make me as desirable as she was. As attractive. As popular. With booze, I'd find a boyfriend, hold hands with him, and go on dates on Saturday nights. Then I'd have something to tell that cadre of girls I'd meet, who would love me and call me to tell me everything and even give me keys to their apartments. Booze would make me one of them. An All-American Girl.

I never went to Cisco's dorm room again. But with him I started a pattern that would continue until I finally *did* follow in my mother's footsteps: Men would teach me how to drink.

When I finally left home, not long after my eighteenth birthday, it was for a guy named Kenneth, a twenty-six-year-old from Singapore who became my first real boyfriend. A bartender at a campus restaurant, he experimented on me during our first night together with every brand of liquor in his fully stocked cabinet. But our affair with drinking became only a one-night stand. After that night, we never drank again. He'd have beer that never got opened in the fridge. He had wine for guests in the pantry, which we forgot about. We chose to eat instead, and I gained thirty pounds before I finally left him for another, different, older, this time American man.

Joe taught me how to drink like an adult. He had the money and class to mentor me about fine dining, gin and tonics, martinis, and good wine. With him I learned to use drinking as a crutch. It intoxicated me enough to convert me into the extrovert I was only pretending to be. To stay in that relationship I had to forget about being shy. I had to go to cocktail parties and laugh at jokes I didn't find funny, and smile and nod and remember people's names. If it was a dry party—a daytime endeavor, a barbeque, a picnic—my lips stayed sealed, and the man in my life shut his mouth, too, not calling for at least a week while he mused on whether I was the right partner for him. I wasn't.

Single again, I dried up, until I met the three girls I'd been looking for my whole life. With women, I drank like my mother—too much and too often—trying my best to indoctrinate myself into a society that age and culture said I belonged in.

I was single and female, and that meant I was a lush. But of course, no one ever calls it that. No one ever acts like drinking every single night to the point of being drunk is anything less than normal—not when you're in your twenties, and certainly not when you're cute. I had found the life I'd always yearned for, the girl's existence I'd always craved: I had been invited into a foursome of females. Hour by hour, we told each other what a rough night we'd had—the fast food we found on our faces when we woke up; how we almost didn't make it home. Every poor decision was a badge of honor, and the worse the decision was—and the more fried food and alcohol it involved—the better. Excessive drinking was the only criterion for admission into this little club, and so I complied. I was known as "the nurser" for drinking far more slowly than they did, and I made up grand tales of debauchery to match theirs. At home alone, I never drank, though I told them I did.

Illness finally saved me from myself. Lupus, an autoimmune disorder, pushed me to face who and what I was. And wasn't. It wasn't just the drink that was fogging my mind, but my own detachment from my true self. When I finally broke away from this group of women, I found myself, the every-once-in-a-while drinker I always was. Not my mother or my father but something in between. A Chinese American Girl.

MOTHER OF ALL SINS

ASRA Q. NOMANI

BORN IN MUMBAI, India, but raised in a split-level in Morgantown, West Virginia, I knew my mother, Sajida, hid a forbidden fruit beneath the kitchen sink, near the Ajax, Handi Wipes, and stone mortar and pestle for kneading dough for roti, or bread.

She allowed its consumption only at parties for friends with names such as Majumder and Nizami. First she set out culinary delights, the meat butchered with a Muslim prayer, making it *halal,* or legal. Then my father, Zafar, plucked the treasure from under the sink: a two-liter bottle of Coke.

That was as hardcore as my parents got. My mother had grown up wearing the black burka, or face veil and gown, a hallmark of puritanical Islam. Literally teetotalers, my parents learned what most Muslims are taught: Alcohol is *haram,* or illegal.

Some of my Suncrest Junior High School classmates drank beer, but I was never tempted. I did my prayers daily, bowing my head to Mecca, reciting the first chapter of the Qur'an, "Al-Fatiha": "Guide us on the straight path." I was a geek, winning female athlete with the highest GPA in my class. At my locker, when the senior class president asked me to the prom, I responded, "I can't."

My one vice: Coca-Cola, which my older brother, Mustafa, and I guzzled like an elixir.

I applied to only one college: West Virginia University, my hometown school, even with its number-one *Playboy* party-school ranking. A neighborhood called Sunnyside sat on a grimy strip where beer sold for 25¢ a pitcher at dive bars. My freshman year, former WVU football player Andre Gist died, crushed in a car that another former WVU football player, Mark Raugh, had sent reeling over an embankment on University Avenue, just up the road from Sunnyside. A jury cleared Raugh. But outside the courtroom, I met Gist's uncle, a Muslim, and received a sobering reminder of the dangers of alcohol.

At nineteen I crossed into the zone of the *haram,* kissing for the first time with my first boyfriend, consummating my relationship, and daring to take a sip of his Guinness. It tasted like automotive oil. Then one night I discovered my drink: Bartles & Jaymes wine coolers, a glorified fruit juice.

Another night, at our family's yellow Formica kitchen table, I confessed to my mother that I was having sex.

She stared at me, yelled, "Stop," and started sobbing.

I wasn't about to confess my drinking. I started living in contradiction between my values and actions, believing alcohol was legal but hiding it. From nineteen until just after my forty-sixth birthday, I lived a lie. A writer, I challenged puritanical edicts, from "honor killings" to gender segregation, but I didn't dare pen a word challenging our ban on alcohol.

Good Girl Beer

So often when people are faced with contradictions, they don't resolve them. In my struggle lies a deeper effort to sort out the true lessons of religion and the contradictions of dogma and practice. In my twenties, I graduated from WVU and then graduate school at American University in Washington, D.C., landing my first job as a reporter at the *Wall Street Journal.* I drank occasionally but never excessively. During an internship with the *Wall Street Journal* in San Francisco, I hung out with staff reporters and editors at Harrington's

Bar and Grill, the city's oldest Irish bar, swapping gossip and war stories. Drinking allowed some of my overachieving rigidity to evaporate so that I could do something really simple: hang out. Finally, I had a visa to coolness.

Still, I continued trying to be the "good girl." The winter of 1992, I jetted to Pakistan to wed a Muslim man I'd met in graduate school. Even though I had dated men who weren't Muslim, I thought a Muslim man was all that was *halal* for me to marry. The marriage lasted just a few months, though, because I couldn't live in peace with the contradiction of a marriage to someone with whom I was incompatible. A therapist told me to do what I wanted, not what I should. And she said, "Have fun."

In pitch-perfect timing during the summer of 1993, I made a new pal in Danny Pearl, another reporter in the Washington, D.C., newsroom of the *Wall Street Journal*, the son of Jewish parents from Israel. Danny's biography was different from mine, but we'd both grown up with a literal sense of kosher in our lives, learning the Jewish and Muslim edicts that we weren't supposed to eat pork.

One day, on our walk home to Dupont Circle, where we both lived, Danny suggested we turn into a dive bar, the Big Hunt. Sitting in a booth, I talked about my dislike of beer. "You haven't had the right beer," Danny said. "You've got to try wheat beer. It's a good-girl beer."

In the dark of that dive bar, Danny ordered me a wheat beer. I took a sip. It was cold. "Hmmmmm," I said. "I like it." Danny smiled. He had converted me to beer and given me a passport into American culture, too. I caroused with Danny and his friends at bars in the Adams Morgan neighborhood. After work we'd head to the Big Hunt and salsa dancing at Planet Fred. On Saturday night, I'd nurse a beer, listening to Danny's band, Clamp.

While I grew comfortable drinking beer, I was careful to keep it from my parents. When they visited me at the apartment I shared with a friend, I lied and said the beer stash was my roommate's. They thought she was a lush. I didn't want to bear the wrath of violating our ban against alcohol and being considered a "bad girl." I continued my social pilgrimage through American culture with Danny as my guide.

I confessed to Danny that I'd never gone to my high school prom because "good girls" didn't go out on dates. That summer Danny helped me throw my first party ever, A Midsummer Night's Dream, where the women wore cheesy recycled bridesmaid dresses, the men wore tuxedos and suits, and couples posed in front of life-size drawings of Caribbean palm trees. It wasn't just a party. It was a keg party. The following winter, he helped me throw my second party. This keg party got so loud that a neighbor threatened to call the police. I smiled triumphantly.

As I entered my thirties and Danny moved away—first to London and then to Paris—I continued to drink regularly, hanging out at bars such as the Fourth Estate with newsroom friends. While on a visit to London, Danny and I ended up at a bar where an Elvis impersonator signed my underwear. I tried hard liquor for the first time on that vacation, experimenting with flavored vodkas.

Back at home I continued breaking taboos. I wore baby-doll dresses that fell midthigh. I started dating openly, one time daring to wear a bikini during a volleyball tournament at a New Jersey beach, my then boyfriend my doubles partner. My father sat in the sand on the sidelines, averting his eyes.

I moved to the *Wall Street Journal*'s New York bureau, and there, just about every night, I got a seat at the table with the cool kids. I drank beer at Fox and Hounds with contrarian folks, such as page-one editor Ken Wells, who went on to write a book about beer in America.

On one level, the drinking was entirely stupid. Rather than exercise during the workweek, I drank with the gang. Most evenings I walked through the door of my apartment in Brooklyn Heights alone, lonely, and tipsy. One night, I peed going up the stairs to my apartment. Some mornings I'd end up at Happy Days, an all-night diner on Montague Street, diving into a breakfast of sausage—pork sausage—and scrambled eggs. As with alcohol, I ended my ban on pork, considered dirty by Muslims.

Shaken to the core after the attacks on September 11, 2001, I started thinking deeply about the contradictions in our Muslim community—what is *halal* and what is *haram*. I was stunned by the response in our Muslim community to reports that some of the 9/11 hijackers partied, drinking alcohol.

"They couldn't be Muslim," I heard folks say. "They drank alcohol."

I was bemused—and annoyed. They couldn't be Muslim because they drank alcohol? What about the fact they had killed thousands of innocent men, women, and children? The rationale reflected a truth inside the Muslim community, which traditionally has five pillars of the faith—proclamation, prayer, pilgrimage, charity, and fasting. But we practiced a virtual sixth pillar that seemed to transcend murder, theft, rape, and other crimes: prohibition against drinking alcohol.

Yet we practiced it with great hypocrisy. When in Pakistan, reporting on the impending war in Afghanistan, I learned that the country's founder, Mohammad Ali Jinnah, had enjoyed scotch. The country's military dictator at the time, General Pervez Musharraf, also appreciated whiskey. In Karachi, Pakistan, a *Rolling Stone* editor assigned me to do a story on sex, drugs, and rock 'n' roll in Pakistan, and I found plenty of it, including alcohol.

For three decades starting with the birth of Pakistan in 1947, the country permitted the sale and consumption of alcohol. But in 1977, attempting to appease conservative elements of society, Pakistan's prime minister Zulfikar Ali Bhutto put prohibitions in place. Weeks later, an ultraconservative military general, Zia-ul-Haq, orchestrated a coup, ushering in an age of rigid, puritanical Islam. The country's extremist Islamic Ideology Council ruled that only non-Muslims, including Hindus, Christians, and Zoroastrians, could get a permit to buy and consume alcohol.

While in Pakistan, I'd leave my hotel room in Karachi and spend the night partying (I mean reporting) with young Pakistani women and men, drinking and dancing. At French Beach, a strip of beach houses outside Karachi, I met a posse of twentysomethings with a special mobile phone number for local bootleggers, supplying them with beer from Pakistan's Murree Brewery. One of those twentysomethings became my boyfriend.

In late January, Danny called from Islamabad to say he would be coming with his wife, Mariane, to Karachi for an interview. I made sure the house I was renting was stocked with beers for my pal.

The next day, January 23, 2002, Danny left for the interview, with plans to return for a dinner that Mariane and I were throwing for new friends I'd made in Karachi. At home, my boyfriend called his bootlegger to deliver bottles of beer. Shortly after Danny's designated meeting time of 7:00 PM, Mariane began calling him, but his phone wasn't working. The beer bottles emptied with the banter of dinner conversation. Mariane grew increasingly worried.

As darkness fell, Danny still hadn't returned. With sunup, I called the Pakistani police. Before they flooded the house, I swept through the rooms, clearing out the litter of empty bottles. They were the last symbols of a night when innocence remained with me. Something deep and dark was now abrew.

As the days passed, I turned once to a swig of Jack Daniel's from a hotel fridge mini-bottle; I needed to numb myself as we searched for my buddy. In the fourth week of our search, the police got a break that we hoped would lead us to Danny. One of the Pakistani locals ordered a bottle of one of Danny's favorite liquors so it would be ready for his return.

Danny never touched the bottle. Five weeks into our search, with a fallen face, a Pakistani police officer told Mariane, "I couldn't bring your Danny home." That night, in the lobby of the Karachi Sheraton, a Pakistani courier had delivered a video, documenting Danny's gruesome murder, to an FBI agent, a strapping Irish Catholic from the bureau's Newark, New Jersey, field office. Danny had gone from drinking wheat beer at the Big Hunt to getting slain, allegedly by the mastermind of the September 11 attacks, Khalid Sheikh Mohammed, or KSM.

The background on KSM was that, while he plotted terrorism, he was quite the partier. Police in the Philippines said that as he planned a transpacific airline bombing plot called Bojinka, he hung out in karaoke bars and go-go clubs, dating dancers and supposedly throwing a party in 1998 to celebrate the tenth anniversary of the 1988 Pan Am flight 103 explosion over Lockerbie, Scotland.

But none of that dimmed KSM's light in the eyes of his followers. And in one moment he slayed my friend with a butcher knife, documenting the tragedy on film for the propaganda video *The Slaughter of the Spy-Journalist, the Jew Daniel Pearl.* At our last meeting with the Pakistani police, FBI agents, State Department officials, and others, we thumbed our noses at extremist Islam: We drank red wine.

To recover, I returned to my hometown of Morgantown, West Virginia, where I went mostly dry, living near my parents. I had a son, conceived in Pakistan, and while I took him on a pilgrimage to Mecca as a three-month-old, I dabbed my finger in a Samuel Adams beer one night and brought it to my son's lips. I didn't want him to live with a sense of the forbidden that I thought was way too exaggerated.

In 2007 I dared to go to my twenty-five-year Morgantown High School reunion at a dive bar in town, Crockett's. I'd gone there as a college student once, slowly sipping a wine cooler. This time I was going to have a beer with cool kids like Lisa McCroskey, just in from Las Vegas. I did. It was just very normal.

Moving again to Washington, D.C., in 2007, I started work as a cultural trainer to the U.S. military and found new drinking buddies. They happened to be of Irish Catholic descent, and during a business trip we ended up at the Brass Monkey in New York. There I learned to drink Guinness, the dark beer I had once rejected. One of my pals recalled a BBC essay that said we had created our own worst aspects of drinking culture. Indeed, there can be merit to drinking. Drinking breaks down social barriers, promotes cross-cultural understanding, and challenges rigidity.

The Mother of Every Evil

The consensus of scholars is clear about the *sharia*, or Islamic law, on alcohol: It's illegal. To arrive at that conclusion, scholars invoke the Qur'an and the *hadith*, or sayings and traditions of Muhammad, the prophet of Islam. Ironically, the English word *alcohol* comes from the Arabic *al-kohl*, originally eyeliner powders but now referring to grains, fruits, or sugars that create intoxicants when fermented.

Muhammad heard Qur'anic revelations and spoke about *sakar*, a "wholesome drink" gotten "from the fruit of the date-palm and the vine," but the verse offered a gentle warning: "Behold in this also is a Sign for those who are wise." There are even claims that the prophets drank wine.

To me, alcohol is not banned outright in the Qur'an, where it is referred to as *al-khamr*, Arabic for "the fermented juice of the grape." The scriptures are not always clear. Is alcohol a "great sin," as one verse (2:219) states? A crime? Merely an impediment to prayer, as the Qur'an warns us: "Approach not prayers with a mind befogged" (4:43)? Or is it "an abomination of Satan's handiwork" (5:91)?

Asghar Ali Engineer, an Islamic scholar in India, maintains that the Qur'an does not use the word *haram* for *khamr*. But while the scriptures may be open to interpretation, the folklore often prevails and is much more direct.

A *hadith* says that Muhammad stepped out of his mosque and saw his son-in-law Ali incensed. Ali gestured to the carcass of a beloved war camel. Also the prophet's cousin, Ali said that an uncle had slain the camel. Muhammad investigated, finding the uncle drunk. The uncle shouted at the prophet, "You and your father are my slaves!" According to the story, the prophet said, "Truly, alcohol is the mother of every evil!"

Another story claims that Muhammad said, "If a large amount of anything causes intoxication, a small amount of it is also forbidden." Thus many Muslims avoid even the small amounts of alcohol included in recipes, toothpaste, and perfume. Ironically, Qur'an translator Abdullah Yusuf Ali supposedly died from drinking on the streets of England.

Rivers of Wine

Could I come to peace with my relationship with drinking? Living with truth on other issues, from sexuality to identity, allowed me to free myself from the duplicities, contradictions, and shame that so often constrain us as Muslims. Following the news in recent years, I felt angry as we went deeper on the path of self-righteousness and indignation at the supposed faults of others.

The men who plotted the kidnapping of my friend did the five daily prayers—the five pillars of my religion—and they renounced drinking alcohol as an act that isn't pious; the men who killed my friend did so in the name of my religion yet cursed anyone who drank alcohol. The man who fathered my baby went to the mosque for his Friday prayers and in his cell phone had the number of a bootlegger, but he did not stand beside me when I brought my baby into the world. He considered me illegitimate in the eyes of my religion because, while foolishly in love, we weren't married when we conceived our baby. Others called me a criminal in the name of Islam for having a baby out of wedlock.

I chafed at the bridle that constrained free will and critical thinking in Muslim society. It made me angry, and the contradictions in how *haram* and *halal* were enforced baffled me. When I went on a pilgrimage to Mecca in the winter of 2003, I knew sobriety and temperance were part of the culture around me. But I also knew that in the land of the birthplace of Islam, Saudi Arabia, men and women sit in their BMW and Mercedes-Benz luxury cars, crossing a bridge into

Bahrain for alcohol, prostitutes, and drugs. It was clear to me that many Muslims lived a different private life away from detection.

The most puritanical societies, including Saudi Arabia, seem to be defined by these contradictions, the letter of the law extremely rigid and dogmatic but the actual practice of the people often violating those edicts. For women particularly, but not exclusively, the restrictions and repression breed not always compliance but rather conflict and dissonance. I lived this way myself from my late teens into my late twenties—a double life, secretly satisfying my curiosities about men while lying to my parents because I knew that I was crossing boundaries that weren't supposed to be crossed. I couldn't live with the lies, deceit, and hypocrisy after my marriage fell apart, when I realized that we aren't meant to suffer so deeply just to deny our true selves and to realize societal, parental, and external expectations for ourselves. I decided then that I wasn't going to live with contradictions in my own life.

In any society governed by oppression and rules that don't make sense, there will be rebellion, even if it's expressed privately. To express such rebellion publicly is to me the sign of a mature individual and a mature society. In my experience, public disclosure allows for healthier expression and resolution. My experiences with the elite in Karachi, my look into the secret consumption of alcohol by Saudis, and my own experimentation revealed to me the inherent contradictions in Muslim society.

Alcohol use is our dirty little secret. How could men and women drink alcohol throughout the Muslim world yet associate the act with a burden of sin so crushing that it is considered "the mother of all sins," birthing all others? This question has had a profound impact on me because it is emblematic of so many contradictions in our community. Places such as Saudi Arabia strictly segregate men and women, but in the Western world, Saudi men and women freely circulate in mixed-gender situations. We argue that Islam is a religion of social justice, but we treat half our population as second-class citizens. Even where Muslim women are allowed to work in the West, the attitudes of segregation still prevail in traditional communities. Even at dinner parties in Morgantown, at venues such as the WVU student union, the Mountainlair, women accept sitting separately from men in rooms marked Sisters Only.

Religious dogma reaches into the most personal corners of our lives. Inside Islam, Muslim leaders, clerics, and scholars interpreted Qur'anic verses to make alcohol forbidden. This association of sin with alcohol makes Muslims feel shame if they dare to drink.

What I've come to believe is that we don't have to ban alcohol to be wise. Some churches ban alcohol based on biblical verse. Others, from the Catholics to the Methodists, accept alcohol as long as we don't get drunk. We Muslims can adopt a similarly pragmatic approach. Or at least not judge those who do drink.

Ironically, for those who make it to heaven, Qur'anic verses promise *kauser,* an Arabic word that means "abundance," and reference "rivers of wine, a joy to those who drink." As one Muslim woman said, "If we will get rivers of wine in heaven, why not a few glasses of wine on Earth?"

To be clear, I'm not advocating drunkenness. We should live in moderation. In January 2010, trying to understand addiction, I went to Alcoholics Anonymous meetings in Reston, Virginia. At the Reston homeless shelter, in a room packed with about fifty AA members, young and old, I heard their poignant stories. I felt their pain as they struggled with addiction to this drink banned in my faith. It made me understand why some folks believe prohibiting alcohol is a wise way to enforce social control. But bans are also a suppression of individual choice.

Drunk with Power

I would argue that in trying to enforce a ban on alcohol, we've actually gotten drunk on the power and control that come with extreme religiosity. To me, addiction comes in many forms. Its most simple form is substance abuse. But on a deeper level, we can get addicted to puritanical interpretations of faith, and that addiction can become so extreme that we seize from others their right to live with dignity, privacy, and personal security.

Asghar Ali Engineer relates an apocryphal tale from the life of the Sufi poet Rumi. One day, the story goes, Rumi was delivering a sermon to thousands of disciples. A drunkard entered the congregation and fell down on the disciples, who started abusing and beating him.

"How dare you enter this religious congregation in a drunken state!" they said. Rumi, the story continues, stopped his disciples and said, "Not this man but you all are drunk. This man who has drunk wine is right now a helpless person, and you are beating him but in fact you all are drunk, drunk with power. Help him instead of beating him."

In that way, many Muslims are drunk on their idea of piety. They cite precedent in the seventh century to punish others for drinking alcohol. They use a *hadith* transmitted by a companion of the prophet's, Abu Hurayrah: "A man who drank wine was brought to the Prophet. The Prophet said, 'Beat him!'"

Abu Hurayrah continues: "So some of us beat him with our hands, and some with their shoes, and some with their garments (by twisting it) like a lash, and then when we finished, someone said to him, 'May Allah disgrace you!'"

In recent years, we've seen the *hadith* on alcohol used as a license to abuse, beat, and even kill those who drink. In January 2011, Muslim militants stormed a hotel in the southern Yemeni city of Sanaa because it served alcohol. They killed two people and wounded twenty.

Later that year, at about eight one evening in September, in the northeastern Nigerian town of Maiduguri, a "beer parlor" was attacked by gunmen from a Muslim radical extremist group, Boko *Haram*. Its name means "Western education is illegal" in the local

Hausa language. The militants shot and killed four people in the "beer parlor."

From Nigeria to Malaysia, this violent opposition to alcohol consumption is part of an ideological continuum that is dangerous and troubling. A saying of the Prophet Muhammad empowers militants to take punishment into their own hands. It goes so far as to claim that God curses those who drink:

> *Allah curses all intoxicants [alcoholic beverages]; [he also curses] the one who drinks it and the one who serves it, the one who sells it and the one who buys it, the one who makes it and the one who asks that it be made for him, the one who delivers it and the one to whom it is delivered.*

IT'S SAID THAT IN the afterlife, the Prophet Muhammad declared, "Every intoxicant is prohibited. God has made a covenant regarding those who consume intoxicants to give them to drink the discharge [of the inhabitants of Hell]!"

> *The folklore on alcohol is frightening. A Muslim website relates this story: A bad woman invited a good man to bad deeds. The man, fearing God, flatly refused. But, determined not to let her prey escape, the woman offered him one of three choices, each one more dastardly than the other: to consume alcohol, to commit adultery, or to murder her child from a previous marriage. If the man refused, she would cry rape. So, after having pondered his predicament, the pious man chose what he reckoned to be the lesser of the three evils. However, upon taking the alcohol, the man became drunk and then, under the influence of his brain-killing beverage, he killed the child and committed adultery with the wicked woman.*

In Malaysia, a moderate multicultural Muslim-majority country where alcohol is easily available to non-Muslims, or about 40
percent of the population, drinking can mean being fined, caned,
or jailed for up to three years, sentenced by the sharia courts set up
to try Muslims for religious and moral crimes. Though prosecutions
are rare, during a 2008 raid, religious authorities caught Kartika Sari
Dewi Shukarno, then thirty-two and a mother of two, drinking beer
at a hotel in the city of Kuantan on December 11. A religious court
sentenced Kartika, a resident of Singapore, to six strokes of a caning punishment, making her the first woman to face caning under
Islamic law in Malaysia. Kartika told Reuters that she declined to appeal her sentence and offered to come back to Malaysia to be caned.
She lost her job at a hospital and started working as a part-time model to pay the bills.

Religious officials took her to a jail outside Kuala Lumpur, where
the sentence was to be carried out. But after a little while, the vehicle
did a U-turn and authorities freed her. "I am speechless," Kartika
told reporters, saying she didn't know if she was going to be caned
or not. "I want to know what my status is. I want a black-and-white
statement from them." Defiant, she said she was prepared to be caned
and dared authorities to cane her in public.

The use of shaming as a means of social control is typical in
Muslim society, and it's used against Muslims who dare to drink. Finally, in a case that horrified me, four young Muslim men in Sydney,
Australia, broke into the home of a Muslim convert, Christian Mar-
tinez, holding him down on his bed and whipping him forty times
with an electrical cord for drinking alcohol. The ideological battle is
only going to get fiercer as reformers challenge doctrine in the faith.
For my part, I rebelled in an appropriate way: I poured myself a glass
(okay, two) of Jacob's Creek shiraz cabernet.

So What?

When I initially got the assignment to write this essay, I couldn't start writing because, as a forty-six-year-old woman, I still hadn't done something: I hadn't come clean to my parents.

In the summer of 2011, an opportunity to come clean arrived unexpectedly. I had moved into a new home in northern Virginia in May and had stopped hiding my bottles of wine and hard liquor. In August, as my mother cooked in the kitchen of my home, I did something I had never imagined I would do: I balanced a crystal red wine goblet in my right hand and took a delicate sip of red wine in front of my mother. I looked toward her.

My mother didn't even raise an eyebrow. She certainly didn't weep and cry, "Stop!" as she had when I confessed to her that I was having sex at age nineteen.

Instead, my mother responded with the dramatic flair I had come to love and appreciate in her. She simply said, "So what?"

I didn't even finish my glass of wine. In the months that followed, I rarely drank in front of my parents, out of respect for their choice. But I had come clean. Even so, it took me months more to write this essay and finish it. I paced myself slowly, because to publicly own my choice to consider alcohol *halal*, instead of *haram*, I had to be prepared for assault from coreligionists, moderate and extreme.

To live with complete authenticity is a challenge to us all. To live with honesty about our beliefs and our actions is difficult in the face of judgment, criticism, and even the threat of censure and violence.

To finish my writing, I worked my copy at Chics 'n' Wings, a sports bar in McLean, Virginia, and sipped a Stella beer. I continued my writing at Old Brogue, an Irish pub in Great Falls, Virginia, a Guinness in front of me. And I went home to my parents, where I could be honest about where I had been.

I have tried to resolve the contradictions in my life, and even though this sort of journey is risky, I know it is the right thing for me to do. But I am also afraid, because the dogmatic are notoriously aggressive and repressive. Despite the risks, I am happy to be writing about coming to the truth about myself. One way to resolve contradiction is to create a delicate balance between safety and risk taking.

At home I found my mother, standing as she often does by the sink. We still used the blue-and-white-striped Handi Wipes. We'd graduated to Mexican tortillas as our roti. No longer did we have Coke under the sink. I realized it wasn't a healthy drink. A bottle of red wine and Godiva chocolate liqueur stood on the counter by the microwave. My mother knew I had had a beer at the Irish pub. With a loving smile, she showed me the wisdom I think all of us need to embrace. "It's your choice," she said, pausing to take a sip of her Lipton tea.

PART 4 FAMILY

DRINKING THE KOOL-AID

"Let's drink together friendly and embrace.
That all their eyes may bear those tokens home
Of our resorted love and amity."
—William Shakespeare, *Henry IV, Part II*

MY FATHER, MY BEER BUDDY

ANN HOOD

MY FATHER, HE DRANK BEER. In our back yard, at beer joints around our sad little town; on hot afternoons and every Friday night, year-round. Drinking beer was one of his greatest pleasures. And I— his only daughter and youngest child—was another. Wherever my father went, I followed. One of my earliest memories is of a summer day, the air heavy with the smell of mowed lawns and fruit ripe on the trees in our yard. My father and my great-uncle Rum are sitting outside on plastic webbed chairs, a cooler of beer between them. They are sharing stories about things I don't understand or care about. My number-one desire is to sit on my father's lap, and without my having to say this, he just *knows*. He scoops me up in one strong motion. One arm stays around me. The other lifts his beer to his mouth and takes a long grateful swallow.

I could not know then, on that long-ago lazy afternoon, that this simple moment would come to symbolize our relationship: For the rest of our lives together, my father knew how I felt and scooped me up into his warm embrace. For all my life with him, beer was on the sidelines. We would toast with it and cry over it and travel the world tasting it together. Every Christmas for the last five years of his life, I gave him a subscription to the Beer of the Month Club. He would wait for me to come home before he tasted the newest delivery. Memory is a strange thing, the way it blurs and morphs events. Maybe on that long-ago afternoon, as I sat on his lap and summer lazily played out around us, he didn't offer me a sip of his beer. But I choose to think he did, that he lifted that cold brown bottle to my lips and I took a tentative sip. I remember him laughing at the look of disgust on my face, and I remember wishing that I would grow up fast and learn to like that malty taste so I could share his love of beer with him. And of course I see the years passing too quickly, all the beers drunk, all the stories and hours we shared gone, my father dead a decade, and me here, that once bitter taste so sweet to me now.

When I close my eyes and conjure my father, the first thing I see is his eyes, so blue that I used to think that if I could climb inside them, I would find the ocean back there. His scent: Old Spice, Vitalis, Gleem. He had teeth as crooked as a broken zipper. He whistled and he hummed and he smiled, showing off those teeth. Psoriasis turned his arms and legs bright red and scaly. At the beach, kids would ask him what was on his skin. "That's syphilis, sweetie," he'd tell them.

For half of my childhood he was in the navy, a six-foot-four Seabee in his white sailor suit, blond hair peeking out from beneath his tilted hat. For the other half, he worked for the IRS, commuting from our small town in Rhode Island to his office in Government Center in Boston by train every day. He wore suits in patterns like Harris tweed, Glen plaid, checkerboard. On Sunday nights he spread the Sunday paper on the kitchen floor, took his shoe shining kit from the hall closet, and lined up his dress shoes: black wing tips, brown loafers, shiny Italian ones. I watched him lay out the various polishes, brushes, and chamois cloths. Then together we would get to work, polishing those shoes until they gleamed.

During that period, when my father ate lunch at fancy restaurants in Boston, he had a flirtation with martinis. One weekend when I was about twelve, he spent an afternoon teaching me how to make a good one. He was a man who liked his juice in juice glasses, his ties hung on a tie rack, hand towels at the bathroom sink. Therefore, martinis required a silver bar set—jigger, shaker, long stirring spoon, and strainer. They required perfect martini glasses, heavy inverted triangles on thin stems. And Tanqueray gin.

My mother didn't drink much at all. It made her weepy and sentimental. So it was I who every afternoon at five thirty took that gin out of the liquor cupboard, where it sat beside my mother's now dusty bottles of Kahlua, cherry Heering, and crème de menthe; got the bar set from its place in the cupboard below; and made my father a shaker of perfectly mixed and chilled martinis. As soon as he walked in the door and loosened his tie, I thrust his drink into his waiting hand.

But despite the martini period, when I think of my father, I think of beer.

My father, Lloyd Hood, was the eighth of nine children. He grew up on a farm in southern Indiana, equidistant from Cincinnati and Kentucky, and he kept a slight Southern drawl his whole life. He could not eat peaches because their fuzz gave him goose bumps. He was suspicious of chestnuts. He put salt on his watermelon and a slice of cheddar cheese on his apple pie. When he made us scrambled eggs on Saturday mornings, he added sugar to them. And when he cooked corn on the cob, he boiled it in milk.

I know all this because I used to study everything he did. Maybe because he was away from home when I was young, stationed in Cuba at Guantánamo Bay, my father seemed mysterious and exciting to me. For almost three years, he was a man in a black-and-white picture that my mother kept on top of the television. While I watched *Lost in Space* and *My Favorite Martian,* I kept one eye on him. He wrote us letters every week in his sprawling, hard-to-decipher handwriting. My mother read them out loud after dinner, pausing from time to time and smiling to herself. "What did he say?" I'd demand, desperate for every syllable, every vowel and consonant he'd sent our way. And when she wouldn't share these private messages with me, I cried jealously.

One morning my mother ordered me to put on my good dress, a black one covered with bright yellow sunflowers. My brother wore madras shorts and a pink shirt. She put sailor hats on both our heads and drove us to Newport, across one bridge and then a ride on a ferry to a dock, where we waved miniature American flags as a destroyer, honking loudly, pulled in. Down a gangplank marched man after man in dress whites. It wasn't until I saw him that I understood why we had come: My father was home at last.

On Wednesday nights my mother chaperoned my brother's weekly junior high dances. I couldn't wait for dinner to end and my brother to descend the stairs in his too-tight blue blazer and clip-on tie. My mother wore a matching skirt-and-sweater set, red lipstick, and a big spritz of Shalimar. I stood at the door with my father, waving goodbye to them as our green Chevy Caprice rolled away. Then my father opened a bottle of Miller beer and sighed happily as I prepared my Easy-Bake Oven. Each week we baked miniature corn muffins, small disks of devil's food cakes, a six-pack of tiny yellow cupcakes under the oven's burning bulb. We slathered on frosting and ate all of it, every crumb.

While we ate, my father worked his way through the other six-pack, this one of beer, and told me stories of his travels. How he ate dog stuffed with rice in Morocco, rancid hundred-year-old eggs in Peking, grape leaves in Greece. He told me there was a tribe in Africa called the Ganji who had black skin and white butts. He had seen it rain on just one side of a street and stay sunny on the other. Once, scuba diving, he came face to face with a moray eel. In China people dropped dead of starvation right at his feet. But if he stopped, he would have to pay to bury them, so he always just kept walking. He had been engaged to a girl in San Francisco, where the fog was so thick it hid buildings and boats. He'd run away from home when he was fourteen and gotten a tattoo of an eagle in front of a red sun. That tattoo was on his left forearm, and I would trace it while I sat on his lap, listening.

Those Wednesday nights helped set my course. A desire to travel, to eat strange things, and to visit mysterious places took hold. Years later, when I graduated from college, I went to work as a flight attendant for TWA and eventually flew over a million miles, collecting my own stories to share with my father over beers. By then I was old enough to drink, too, and he would wait for me by the kitchen door when I came home to visit, the beers cooling in the fridge, ready to hear my adventures. My mother grew bored easily and would listen politely for a while before picking up a dustcloth or disappearing into the kitchen. But my father and I sat and talked, pausing only to get up for another beer. He indulged my newly acquired sophisticated taste and bought St. Pauli Girl or Guinness. The only thing that really changed as I grew older was that I took the role of storyteller. But it was a skill I had learned from him. He would open two bottles of beer and hand me one, then lean back in his chair. "And then what happened?" he'd ask, and I would tell him everything.

For my entire childhood, my mother played cards every week with a group of thirteen women who called themselves the Dirty Dozen. After dinner she'd dress up in one of her matching skirt-and-sweater sets, gather her coffee can full of pennies and two packs of Pall Malls, and go to one of their houses. Every thirteen weeks they came to our house. When that happened, I had to stay up in my bedroom. I wasn't allowed to eat any of the special food my mother made for the Dirty Dozen—triangles of crescent roll dough stuffed with hamburger meat and water chestnuts, chicken baked with apricot jam and Russian dressing, lemon meringue and chocolate cream pie.

My father went out on Friday nights with Uncle Rum. Uncle Rum was my grandmother's cousin, and he lived in an apartment behind our house with his unmarried sister and brother. He smoked stogies and took baths at a public bathhouse in Providence every Saturday. He and my father drank beer on Friday nights, at a bar called Vic's or down the hill at the German Club, a place that smelled of spilled beer and sawdust, where my father sometimes took my brother and me on Sunday afternoons. He would sit at the bar drinking beer with Uncle Rum and neighborhood men with names like Two-Tumbler and Brownie while we drank Cokes and played on the bowling or pinball machines.

The day my father consumed the most beer was on his birthday, the Fourth of July. He would rise at dawn and play John Philip Sousa marches as loud as our stereo could go. The beer he'd put on ice the night before would be perfectly cold, and he began to drink as soon as he got up. He marinated shish kebabs, formed patties out of hamburger meat, split buns, stirred the pot of baked beans. Inside, my mother swore and grumbled in her nightgown. She did not like parties or crowds. She did not like beer. By noon our street could not hold any more cars, and guests blocked our neighbors' driveways or parked on their lawns. "The Stars and Stripes Forever" played. Cases of beer were consumed, and drunken men put pots and colanders on their heads, hoisted brooms to their shoulders, and marched around the block. At night we kids ran around barefoot with sparklers, my mother by then usually so mad that she refused to come outside. Roman candles and bottle rockets sent smoky squiggles of blue and pink and green into the inky sky. At some point the police were called. Sometimes they took the beer my father offered them, stood on the sidewalk with him, and watched the burst of yellow light.

After Uncle Rum died, I became my father's Friday night date. At first I was too young to drink beer with him. But we would go to Freddie's Pizza or Lum's for hot dogs, or to the Ground Round, where we threw our peanut shells on the floor and ate cheeseburgers on rye buns. He always gave me a few sips of his beer. I liked the taste by then, the foam followed by the cold sharp beer. After I turned eighteen, we ordered pitchers of beer with our dinner. I still asked for his stories, and I still loved the sight of his starting-to-fade tattoo peeking out from his flannel shirtsleeve.

He was the only father who made the thirty-mile drive to my college pub on Friday nights. Perhaps I was the only daughter who wanted her father there. He would buy my friends and me pitchers of beer and listen to our love problems. He gave us advice: "A stiff dick has no conscience," he'd say, which made us blush. But soon enough we understood that he was right. More than once on a weekend night, I found myself at Twin Willows or the Bonnet Lounge having had too much to drink. *Never ever drink and drive,* my father had taught me. I would go to the pay phone, put in a dime, and tell him I'd had too many beers. Then I would sit outside in the cool salty air and wait for him to pull up in the parking lot. He never scolded me. Instead, he thanked me for calling instead of getting behind the wheel.

One of my greatest pleasures when I got older was taking my father to beer halls in Europe. Since I was a flight attendant for TWA, my parents got free passes to fly anywhere TWA flew. We traveled to Europe together frequently, and my mother joined us for the usual tourist sites. The geometry of my family was such that my father and I had our beer drinking together and my mother and I went shopping together, with the three of us doing everything in between. The three of us climbed the narrow stairs at the Anne Frank House and oohed and ahhed as the lights turned golden in the Grand-Place. But at the end of the afternoon, my father and I headed to the beer halls. My mother sometimes came along, ordering coffee from the bewildered waitresses. Other times she went back to the hotel for a nap, her own favorite indulgence. In Amsterdam my father and I spent a day at the Heineken brewery; in Munich we drank steins of beer and sang along with the oompah bands; in Brussels we drank our beer and ate *moules frites.* These trips brought together the things my father and I shared most: beer and a love of travel. During these years, instead of telling each other stories, we were creating our own—adventures we shared. Later, after I stopped flying for TWA and my father's health kept him from traveling, our evenings over beers became a vehicle for remembering our afternoons drinking beer in foreign cities.

My father retired before my mother did, and with free time, he started to drive to New York City, where I lived, to spend a few days with me. Just like when I was a little girl, I would wait for him by the door. When I heard the elevator ding at my floor, and the doors slide open to reveal my father with his leather overnight bag, whistling through his crooked teeth, my heart would soar like it always did at the sight of him.

Now I showed him new things. I took him to East Sixth Street for Indian food and to Szechuan Gourmet. I taught him how to eat sushi, how to mix the wasabi in the soy sauce, how to use chopsticks to lift the roll and dip it in. When I discovered McSorley's Old Ale House on East Seventh Street, I couldn't wait to bring my father there. He arrived in New York City one winter night, the wind blowing hard and cold. This was before emphysema made it impossible for him to walk much. The two of us set off from my Bleecker Street apartment. "You are going to so love this place," I said, my hand in his big leather-gloved one. McSorley's is the oldest Irish tavern in New York City and one of the last of the "men only" pubs, admitting women only after legally being forced to do so in 1970, only a dozen years earlier.

My father fell immediately in love with the place, its sawdust floors and cranky bartenders, its eponymous beer. "Oh, Poops," he said, using his old nickname for me, "this is our kind of place, isn't it?" We clinked glasses, and I eagerly showed off all the secret treasures of the bar—the Houdini handcuffs attached to the bar rail, the wishbones hanging above the bar, placed there by boys going off to World War I. "A good bar has a lot of stories to tell," my father said appreciatively.

"Like us!" I told him.

"Like us," he said, holding his glass up to mine.

Without my noticing, time passed. My father had been a heavy smoker for most of his life, but in 1989 he quit cold turkey and never lit up again. A few years later he started to get pneumonia every autumn. Sometimes he'd get a second bout in winter. Over time his breathing became labored. His doctor diagnosed asthma, and he carried an inhaler in his shirt pocket, puffing on it several times a day. On a trip to San Francisco with my mother and me, he was unable to walk quickly one afternoon as we hurried to catch a bus. Instead he sat on a low wall, unable to catch his breath. This time the doctor diagnosed emphysema. When we went out on a Friday night date, I found myself watching him carefully, as if I could spot and ward off anything bad that might come his way.

On Labor Day weekend in 1996, my father and I went to an annual Greek Festival. By then I had moved back to Rhode Island and was nine months pregnant with my second child. When I couldn't find a parking place, I dropped my father at the festival entrance. Embarrassed, he said he couldn't bear making me walk far when I was pregnant. "Maybe we should just go home," he said, shaking his head sadly. But I insisted we go inside and eat souvlaki and baklava and that he drink beer enough for both of us, like we always did. I see now that I could not accept what was happening. But when after less than an hour he lay his head on a picnic table and said that maybe I should take him to the ER, I touched his forehead with the quarter-size dent in it from a long-ago mishap during a game of kick the can, and his skin burned hot beneath my hand. I knew that another pneumonia had come.

Something in me shifted that night as I sat by his side, waiting for the doctor to come and tell us what we already knew. I cannot say I knew then what was waiting around the corner. I can say only that I began that night to prepare for bad news. It came two days later. My father's doctor looked at the chest X-rays taken that night in the ER and saw a spot on his lungs. That spot turned out to be terminal lung cancer. That cancer killed my father exactly six months later.

My father wanted to live. He agreed to radical chemotherapy and radiation in the hopes of beating this thing. I read the statistics and I talked to friends who were doctors, and I understood that he was not going to win.

The Friday night before he began the course of treatment that would speed up his dying instead of saving his life, we went out to our favorite barbecue joint. We ordered pitchers of beer and whole racks of St. Louis ribs. It was a warm October night, but my father, as always, wore long sleeves to hide the psoriasis on his elbows. Still, I could see his tattoo, now faded enough to blur the images, the eagle just a soft blue, the sun a muted pink. I asked him to tell me what that dog stuffed with rice tasted like in Morocco. I asked him what a moray eel looked like up close. He told me his familiar stories, and I listened, memorizing them, memorizing the sound of his voice and the blue of his eyes.

Every day since my father died, on April 14, 1997, I've missed him. He taught me how to tell a good story. He gave me a love of travel and the bigger world. He showed me what it felt like to be loved, truly loved. And he taught me how to drink beer. "Always get the good stuff," he told me. "It not only makes a good impression, but it tastes better, too." He used to sing a song that said in heaven there is no beer; that's why we drink it here. But I hope there is beer there, because surely my father is in heaven, and I want him to have pitchers of the good stuff, lots of it, always. As for me, every time I take a sip of a cold one, I imagine him sitting across from me, smiling. I always pause to lift my glass upward in a toast, hoping he can see me still.

KIDS, THANK YOU FOR POT SMOKING

JACQUELYN MITCHARD

THE RECREATIONAL DRUG that I would choose for my three teenage daughters and my three young-adult sons would be nothing.

Nothing would be a great choice for their health and their sanity. And it would be great for *my* sanity. Let's not forget my needs.

However, evidence suggests that I am dealing in fantasy. Evidence suggests that they *will* drink, and not just a tot of prosecco on holidays. Evidence suggests that they will swill a bucket of beer, if not the first chance they get, then shortly thereafter. That being the case—hold on to your mug—my second choice, after nothing, would be marijuana.

Don't get the wrong idea. I don't encourage them to smoke dope. I actively discourage them. However, if the choice were mine, I would rather that they smoke dope than drink booze. Any kind of booze.

Ever.

What am I, nuts?

Yes, I am, when it comes to the subject of drinking.

I'm the dry flower of a blooming family tree of alcoholics. The band at weddings used to call my intelligent, artistic, and beautiful mother Mrs. Robinson when she got tanked up and flirtatious. After that, when her mascara ran, she was a sad clown and dangerous to be around, especially for someone who loved her and believed what she said. When I was nineteen and she was fifty-one, all that ouzo and the three packs of Salems a day demanded their toll, and she died.

She left me with my dad.

My dad was hardly an advertisement for the pluses of sobriety. He was known to mistake his best friend for an adversary and, having the strength and personality of Jake LaMotta, once put said friend through a TV. Another time my father beat my mother so badly that he broke her eyes, nose, and cheek. Once he went looking for her with his police special revolver.

When I was little, I suspected but wasn't sure that most families did not spend Christmas Eve drinking and dancing, then drinking and flirting, then drinking and fighting. One year I asked my mother, "Please, can nobody get drunk tonight?"

Horrified, she stopped in her black silk and stilettos, figuratively although not literally flat-footed. She said, "But that's what everybody does. What else would we do? Otherwise it wouldn't be any fun!" She put on a TV channel that played Christmas carols against the backdrop of a stocking-bedecked fireplace. "Here," she said. "Watch this."

On Christmas morning my little brother came to sit in my bed while we waited for my parents to get up so we could see what Santa had brought. The lights glittered, the decorations were as festive as any at a florist shop, but Dad needed black coffee and a Bloody Mary before we could open our presents. It was often late, nearly afternoon.

One New Year's morning, when I was eleven and my brother five, my grandparents dropped us back home—we'd stayed with them overnight while my parents were at a house party at the estate of their wealthiest friends. It turned out, though, that the party was just beginning. My parents didn't come home for two more days, and something warned me that I shouldn't share this with my grandparents (who had left for Florida anyway) or the neighbors who lived near our apartment. We were safe. We watched TV; we ate Campbell's tomato soup and Good Humor bars. When my parents returned, exhausted and bedraggled, looking as if they'd spent two days stranded in a train station, my mother warned me with a look that their tardiness, like so much else, was nothing we would ever speak of again.

Every day was a holiday when it came to drinking. And as I grew older, I was still frightened and hurt, but also ashamed, when my mother, with increasing anger and desperation, called my father over and over, asking him to come home from work. He was the only one who knew how to mix the martinis.

Although he grieved after my mother died, my father liked the ladies. When he was drinking, he would entertain, leaving my fourteen-year-old brother literally barred outside the apartment in the back stairwell. (Dad installed the kind of huge hasp that keeps bulls in barns.) There were times when our father forgot altogether that he had a son, and my kid brother slept on the stairs after finishing his algebra.

My brother married very young.

My grandparents on my mother's side, as well as my aunts and uncles, loved a cocktail as well. There were a great many affairs between mothers and their daughters' husbands—and the other way around. Adding to the drama, card games erupted into fistfights, father to son and brother to brother.

We weren't even Irish.

Although I tried dutifully to be a party girl, I went to college and became, in the words of my best friend (who still says this), the most boring girl on Earth. Since I didn't drink and never really got into the habit of smoking, I often wandered into the bedroom and read books at parties or curled up alone on the coats and took a snooze.

The years didn't change anything. As one of my older children said, I never learned to hold my liquor, except at arm's length. What's truer is that I never saw anything good come of drinking.

Not then. Not later. Not now.

When I was a child, a young man who worked for my father was a volunteer firefighter whose habit was steak, eggs, and a brew or five when he got off his shift in the early dawn. Once he hit a curb and wrecked his knee. Once he hit a kid and wrecked his life. The little boy didn't die, but he needed repeated surgeries to walk again. The firefighter lost his jobs, his family, his home and became . . . a drunk. Everything he had went to repairing the life of the child and his large family, which could never be repaired.

One of my older son's best friends had not one but two older brothers in rehab. When all three boys were little, their dad was disabled in a drunk-driving accident, and he used that opportunity to take up drinking full-time.

It's not just boys, though, and it never was.

A few years ago a neighbor's daughter was left by a guy on the side of the road, drunk but unhurt, without a coat, within walking distance of her house. She passed out and never woke up. The guy went to prison for a while. But the girl's family is doing a life sentence.

Senator George McGovern's daughter Terry was a devoted mom and a sincere person. On a December night she walked home from a bar and froze to death in a snowbank.

I could go on forever.

I'm a crank when it comes to drinking. The equivalent of the kind of person who writes letters to the editor all the time. But I find it impossible to repent. I live in a social setting in which people are as deep in denial about drinking as they are into drinking.

Perhaps it is true that a certain sparkling grace comes from one glass of champagne, as author James Cain once wrote. Then there is the certain gross, shambling, maudlin belligerence that comes from four or twelve glasses of anything. There is the puking, the stink, and worst of all that tree that leaps out of nowhere, the punch or the gun that ends a fight, a romance, a job, a life. Kids don't drink to act like James Bond. They drink to behave like James Dean.

I understand that part.

What I don't understand is my peers' attitude toward booze and the young . . . or booze altogether.

As a newspaper reporter, I did the inevitable story about a country come-from-behind kid, a soon-to-be cager who went not to Indiana University but to the cemetery with two of his teammates. Another teammate will spend his life in a robotic wheelchair.

When I interviewed the family for the story, I didn't have to search for empathy. Then the mother of a young teen, I found it nearly impossible to speak. But the lost lad's granny, one of those country souls who could wring a chicken's neck while reciting a Bible verse, said to me, "Well, you can't blame him. It's the same thing we did, of course. My husband and I used to drive those roads with our friends with a big bucket of beer on ice in the trunk. He just got unlucky is all."

The sixteen-year-old had been dead for seven hours. It was one of those stories for which I left out the best quote, to protect fools.

Many of my same-age pals have teen or college-age children, as do I. They don't say the same thing as that boy's granny, but their attitude is not profoundly different. Not all but many of my friends allow their underage children to drink with them—at dinner, evenings at home, in restaurants, and on holidays. They want them to learn to "handle" drinking. They want them to learn "how to drink," as though drinking were a necessary part of adulthood, like driving or taking the ACT test.

These friends think I have a screw loose. A cocktail is "fun," they point out. Wouldn't it be hypocritical, they ask me, for them to forbid their kids the same pleasure they enjoy?

Well, presumably they enjoy a good romp in the hay, too. But they aren't eagerly anticipating the day when their young people try different sexual partners as they try different microbrews. They don't want to *help* their kids learn to have sex at home (or if they do, they don't tell me).

I'm the nonconformist in this setting. Perhaps especially in the Midwest, where I come from, there is no occasion—from a ball game to a baptism—that is complete without tying one on. At their wedding, a young relative of mine and her groom rented a bus to transport them and their friends from the church to the reception hall, so they could safely and privately get drunk on the way. Their wedding planner came up with the idea.

Moreover, my friends add, pot is *illegal*—as though those billboards that read PARENTS WHO HOST RISK THE MOST are referring to serving scrambled eggs.

Well, darn it. They're right. Pot is illegal. And it's expensive. It should be illegal and expensive. Being stoned isn't a great idea. Driving stoned is a truly hideous idea, and I will never, ever condone it. It's just the safer alternative. A close pal's kid lost his license for a year for driving under the influence of marijuana. Good for him. He won't do that again.

Of course, people overuse and abuse marijuana. But the *Reefer Madness* movie I saw in high school (yes, either I am that old or my school was that lacking in creativity) was a big lie. Pot smokers don't litter the world with hit-and-run corpses. If they do, the Centers for Disease Control and Mothers Against Drunk Driving don't know about it.

Medical and psychological experiments have repeatedly found that marijuana has a less dramatic impact on driving ability than alcohol does. Perhaps because smoking dope is still a hidden thing, and one that cops are less likely to be understanding about, pot smokers tend to be more aware of their impairment. And according to a 2010 paper published in the *Journal of Psychoactive Drugs,* stoned drivers slow down, whereas drunk ones speed up. Even information from Students Against Destructive Decisions (SADD), which sponsors a program called Steer Clear of Pot, points out that the effect of pot is "shorter" and less "profound."

In a 2010 issue of *Psychology Today,* Jann Gumbiner, PhD, writing on teenagers' mind-set, points out: "The large majority . . . try marijuana and never become addicted. . . . People can quit rather easily." She adds, "It is much harder to quit smoking [cigarettes] than it is to quit smoking pot."

I don't necessarily buy any of this as gospel truth. But the body count from stoned drivers just isn't there. However, I do think that smoking dope addles your brain, if the behavior I've witnessed involving my college-age son, his best friend, and a golf cart is any proof.

Yet pot smoking isn't part of a public social scene. Drinking is. Whole vacations are based on drinking (wine country; Oktoberfest). Beer is the drink that made Milwaukee famous. It's what those beautiful draft horses are pulling in the wagons framed by snow and holly wreaths in countless Christmas commercials. Disaronno liqueur commercials suggest that the beverage renders both the woman at the bar and the bartender deeply sexy—and this is probably true, especially after a certain hour and a certain amount of Disaronno. Colt 45 malt liquor is even more baldly suggestive, and if you drink rum, hey, an island with paper lanterns, balloons, and gorgeous exotic girls who dance like Beyoncé will appear on that magical island in the ocean, or the lake . . . or even a puddle. All that romping and sensual delight, not to mention good old American "fun" and even yupscale culturality, are not only acceptable but downright alluring.

Not so much with pot. Pot is purchased in grubby ways from sketchy people.

EVEN THOUGH I LIVE IN one of the havens of marijuana overuse, akin to Boulder, Colorado, where gray-haired gents with PhDs light up big blunts, this isn't a usual life pattern for the mature. There are no "pot tasting" events at local restaurants or "micro-harvest" burger joints that feature joints. Although, as my hippie pals righteously point out, pot comes from the ground (as do malt, hops, wine grapes, juniper berries, potatoes, and most other stuff that goes into fermenting booze of all kinds), it's still vaguely "underground." In the end, that's a big, big part of what I favor about dope.

In general, unless you're really devout, you outgrow smoking dope. Very few forty-year-old mommies and daddies fire up a big blunt, unless it's for a tenth-anniversary giggle (literally). You grow out of dope. But you grow into booze.

When you turn twenty-one, drinking becomes magically legal. My brother, whose basement bar rivals Joe Allen's, gave each of my sons a case of Spotted Cow when he turned twenty-one. (I bought it from each of them, at an inflated price. Okay, I know, I know, that's going too far.) The front of the birthday card read: "A guy walks into a bar." You opened it and it read inside: "At last!" Hooray! No more subterfuge but a great many breath mints. Designated drivers, or so we hope. The cast party. The pub crawl. The postsoftball belly-up.

Fast-forward ten years. You develop a better tolerance. The nightly glass of wine. The Friday six-pack. Sundays with football. Tuesdays with tennis. Every day's a good day to drink.

Fast-forward ten more years. You graduate from beer to martinis. If you have a drinking "problem," this is the age when you'll start to deny it. If you're an alcoholic, you already look it. Your skin has too many burst veins. You've got a little gut. You've embarrassed your kids. And if your spouse doesn't like to drink, well, then you're on your own.

All this—and it is preachy—is only a theory carried out in the region of my desk. However, my kids' friends who were big drinkers are *still* big drinkers. They're bigger drinkers. My oldest son is now twenty-seven, and what he calls "that stuff" (read: pot) is starting to wear out for him. It's incompatible with a real job and a real life, as he puts it, unless you're an actor.

Yet the younger two, twenty-one and twenty-four, still smoke dope a few times a month. More than I'd like. One of them calls his weekly stone "transcendental medication," a phrase I find more annoying than clever.

Still, all three have graduated college. So far as I know—and I surely do not know it all—smoking pot hasn't interfered with anything, at least so far. I know that if my daughter, a high school sophomore, hasn't tried smoking pot, she has friends who have, and soon she will. The thought turns my stomach, as does the thought of her chugging a beer. I worry even more about the possible sexual implications of lowered inhibitions.

Okay, I'll hand it to you—this is a rant.

I've been absolutely smashed exactly twice in my life, once to the detriment of my boyfriend's beautiful new brown leather coat. The other time I was horsing around with my brother after drinking a glass of hot mulled wine, and we fell off a bench. After both those incidents, I felt worse than I'd ever felt from a virus. For my kids, "the time Mom got drunk" lives in infamy. They'll never let me forget it.

If you press me hard enough, I'd say get rid of the guns along with the booze. Anarchy! Disorder! Tradition destroyed. Granted, also, my kids might turn out to be fat, sloppy, unmotivated losers who could never work in series TV, consuming far greater than their share of the world's available Doritos. My brother has the same family history as I, but he makes his own beer and his kids are high-achieving athletes and scholars. I'm not a normal person in this recreational regard, and I don't expect others to fall into my ranks.

(If they did, however, the world would be a better place.)

MY FOREIGN LEGACY

CAREN OSTEN GERSZBERG

THE PHOTO SITS ON THE desk in my office. In it, the sky is gray with clouds, hovering over the sandy banks of the Loire River, where my mother and I sit on a small blanket. She's wearing a transparent white blouse with a long strand of pearls, and I'm dressed in a sleeveless navy top with patchwork jeans. Our picnic spread consists of a baguette, fresh peaches, some smelly cheese I won't touch, and some dark chocolate I will. There's a bottle of red wine for her, a *jus d'orange* for me. I am seven years old in the photo—snapped by a local fisherman—during a week in which my mother guided me through Paris, her native city, and on a side jaunt to the châteaux of France's Loire Valley.

Fast-forward thirteen years, and my mom and I are again ambling through the French countryside. This time I'm twenty. The tall, bright sunflowers, thirsty for the summer rays, line the route on which we drive our white Peugeot rental car. Each night of our ten-day journey we spread out a map on the bed to plot the following day's destination. We call ahead to book a room in a *relais*, or inn, and the next morning begin to make our way toward our final destination, the southwestern city of Toulouse. During World War II, my maternal grandparents were deported to concentration camps—and survived. But my mother and her sister were given refuge in Toulouse, hidden by nuns in a Franciscan convent near the city center.

Along the way we pause in quaint villages for lunch or a *café crème*, but more often we pick up food at local markets for a picnic lunch. When hunger strikes, we pull over alongside one of those inviting sunflower fields, throw down a blanket, and set up our meal. No matter what we eat, we wash it all down with long sips of red wine. We don't always have cups, so we often savor the locally made wine straight from the bottle.

Sitting on a picnic blanket in the French countryside with my mother was pure joy—at both age seven and age twenty. During the second trip, our lunches were filled with discussions about my life and hers, the growing complexities for me as a young adult, the middle-aged challenges for her, the future for us both. I felt as if I could tell her anything. We weren't just enjoying life, we were sharing a piece of her heritage that I'd already embraced with gusto—the language, literature, culture, and lifestyle, and of course the wine.

GROWING UP WITH A FRENCH mother was different. She had an accent that I wasn't always proud of, and she had unusual habits, such as blasting opera at high volume throughout the house and sunbathing topless—not just on the beaches in Cannes but also on our back porch. A green-tinted glass bottle filled with chablis was always chilling in the fridge, and on the shelf below rested a glass plate that held four or five imported cheeses. For my brother and me, there was an ample supply of tiny little squares of La Vache Qui Rit cheese (known to most as the Laughing Cow). My parents drank wine at every meal, and when I went to bed, I said *bonne nuit* rather than good night.

At least once a month, my parents got together with their mostly European friends for dinner parties, Sunday afternoon card games, or barbecues. We kids were always included in these lengthy gatherings. We listened to the music and singing (one of my dad's pals played the accordion) and observed the dancing and drinking. The meals lasted for hours, and by dessert time, empty bottles of wine and liquor were strewn across the table. The adults, many of whom I addressed as "aunt" and "uncle," belted out songs in a half dozen languages. The festivities would go on so late that I'd eventually find a couch or bed to curl up on, only to be carried to the car by my dad in the middle of the night for the drive home.

Growing up in surroundings where alcohol was present and enjoyed, but not abused, paved the way for my own drinking habits. As soon as I was of drinking age, I gave no thought to drinking with meals, at bars, during parties, yet I never felt the urge to get rip-roaring drunk. A slight buzz satisfied me just fine, and any time I drank enough to wake up with a hangover, it came with a clear "that was so not worth it" realization.

After several failed relationships, I was fortunate to find a man who not only shared a Holocaust background (he could relate to my family's craziness) but also loved to party. I remember wintry Sunday afternoons early in our marriage when we'd watch all three *Godfather* movies and warm up with a bottle of red wine. We went to the West Village on the third Thursday of every November for a burger and the newly released beaujolais nouveau. When we traveled to Brazil, we fell in love with the Brazilian "national drink," the caipirinha—still my favorite cocktail. And in Barcelona we rested our weary feet with a tapas meal that lasted for hours, accompanied by one (or was it two?) bottles of a Spanish *rosado*.

Parenthood changed our lives but not our love of making life just a little bit more fun—with drink. Though I didn't consume wine while breastfeeding (well, maybe just a little), a green-tinted glass bottle continued to chill in our fridge as it had in my childhood home. Around the same time, however, things in my parents' house began to shift. My father started having difficulty keeping enough wine in the house for my mother's escalating drinking habit.

In 1996, when my mother was sixty-two, her mother passed away. It was the first time I'd ever seen her truly depressed. Losing her mother again, this time for eternity, brought up my mother's childhood trauma and sent her to a dark place. Alcohol became the most effective and "acceptable" way to numb her pain.

Her glass of white wine followed her wherever she went—around the house, from the kitchen to her office, into the bedroom, and of course out at restaurants. It even went with her on train trips to Boston, where my brother then lived, and on car rides to visit friends.

THOUGH I WAS WORRIED about my mom's drinking, my life as a writer and mother of young kids was harried and hectic, and I looked forward to sipping my own glass of wine, particularly when cooking dinner. Often, I pictured my mother when she was my age, clutching a wineglass, standing in her kitchen—the heart of my childhood home—sautéing vegetables, poaching pears, or grating a chunk of gruyère cheese for her homemade onion soup. For me, the habit of simultaneously sipping and cooking was comfortable. Natural.

By the time my father was diagnosed in 2003 with inoperable colon cancer, my mother's drinking had morphed into need and began to steal her away, too. During his numerous hospital stays, I'd visit daily and often find my mother lying in bed alongside my father, usually passed out. She carried a tote bag everywhere she went, and its contents always included a bottle of wine and, in time, vodka.

My mom's drinking made her angry. I tried hard to shield my children from her erratic behavior, but it was difficult, since part of her pattern involved leaving voice messages on our home answering machine, screaming and crying for me to call her back. One day, during a walk to school, my then-five-year-old son asked, "Mom, why do you and Néné fight so much?"

"We sometimes disagree, like all people," I explained, brokenhearted. "But no matter what, she's my mother and I'll always love her."

SINCE MY FATHER'S DEATH in 2006, my mother has only grown more depressed. She was kicked out of one retirement community because of her drinking and the tirades and wacky behavior that ensued. At holiday meals at my house, she has gulped from the drinks of my friends who've gone to the bathroom or turned their heads for a moment. When confronted, she denies she has, or has ever had, a problem.

After my son's graduation from elementary school in spring 2011, my family, including both my mother and my mother-in-law, attended a celebration lunch at a local restaurant. There was a mix-up with our reservation, and they needed to set up another table for us. By way of apology, the maître d' sent over a tray of champagne glasses, filled to the rim with sparkling prosecco. I immediately leaned forward to block my mother's view and told the waiter we'd be declining but were grateful for the gesture. At that moment my seemingly placid mother jumped out of her seat and reached across my body to grab one of the flutes from the waiter's tray. I pried it out of her grasp, handed it to the stunned waiter, and demanded she sit down. The mood, once celebratory, became thick with embarrassment and tension. Needless to say, it was a very long lunch.

Like my mother, I love my wine. But, sadly, it has become loaded with the worry that one day I will like it too much—and need it like she did. Because that dread has taken up residence in my mind, I don't enjoy wine the way I used to. I watch my intake, limit the frequency, and try hard not to pour a glass of wine as a way to ease pain or stress.

My mom's drinking has also affected the way I parent. While I grew up in the midst of a laissez-faire, booze-it-up European setting (I will never forget getting drunk at age fourteen on whiskey sours at my father's fiftieth birthday party), I chose to approach my teenage daughters with a "drinking talk" once they started going to high school parties. I've actually sat on our living room couch and heard myself say things like, "Never drink something that you didn't pour yourself" and, "Don't ever get into a car with someone who's been drinking. We'll pick you up anywhere, anytime." But I'm a product of my upbringing and have also told them, "Just hold a beer if you want to look like you're drinking, and no one will know."

The very notion of limiting alcohol consumption or needing to make conscious decisions around drinking is foreign to me. For me, drinking was an all-out good thing. Not something to worry about, keep away from, or even indulge in. It was pure fun. But I now understand that limits can be useful. Knowledge is power. And I believe it's helpful for my children to understand the nuances of my mother's cultural custom-turned-addiction.

My daughters, now sixteen and eighteen, have unfortunately seen it all. Perhaps knowing that someone as capable, smart, and talented as their grandmother can slide down that slippery slope will give them an insight that I never had.

For them, drinking may never be carefree. When they were younger, I protected them from much of the anguish and spared them the exposure as best as I could. But now the elephant in the room is too big to hide.

After my son's graduation lunch, my eldest daughter turned to me and said, "I felt bad for Simon today. I think it's the first time he ever saw Néné act that way."

Once again, I was heartbroken. For my son. For my mother. For my daughters. For me.

LIKE FATHER, LIKE DAUGHTER?

LIZA MONROY

ONE NIGHT WHEN I WAS a senior in college and visiting my mother, a U.S. diplomat in Greece, we went to a nightclub to hear a band. She ordered a glass of white wine and dumped ice cubes in it. I ordered my drink of choice, a sickly sweet mixture of amaretto and orange juice.

Because of my mother's career, I went to high school in Mexico City, where alcohol was socially permissible once you were "tall enough to reach the bar." I had my first drink at age fourteen, when after-school *comidas*—lunch parties—had open bars and very little food.

My mother knew that my friends and I drank, and there wasn't much parents could do to stop it other than lock up their teenagers or send them to boarding school. She wasn't happy about it, but she didn't want to send me away, either. So she chose to trust me to, as the ads say, "drink responsibly."

Amaretto and OJ was hardly a potent cocktail, but when I finished the first and tried to beckon to the waiter for a second, my mother looked at me sternly and said no. It wasn't the first time she'd cautioned me about alcohol. I didn't order the drink. I knew that if I did, she would worry, and I would hear about it for the rest of the evening.

"It's genetic, you know," she said. She feared that I might turn into my father.

My father was an alcoholic. According to all the research, there's an increased risk of alcohol abuse if you have a parent with alcoholism.

Still, in my teens and early twenties, I was a carefree drinker. I didn't consider my own drinking habits in relation to my father's. My drinking as a young adult was, I think, typical. In college I got drunk on cheap white zinfandel with my girlfriends by the Charles River in Boston on warm nights. I snuck into bars and clubs and had a couple of vodka cranberries. Mimosas were nice at brunch. I drank consistently but not excessively. I didn't think about addiction. I could be okay with or without a drink; I just preferred life *with* drinking.

My mother's stern warnings must have lodged in my brain and lain dormant during my young-adult years, only to come out in my thirties as a voice I can't seem to shake.

My father's story haunts me. He started out with such promise. No one could have predicted the dark place his road would lead to. This is at the heart of my fear: At one point, he too was enjoying only a drink or two to unwind after work.

My father, a tall handsome Italian, adored me. As a toddler, I would affix myself to his leg like a little monkey when he had to go to work at the restaurant where he waited tables in Seattle. He would walk around the house like that, his foot just big enough to support my small bottom. As he went about getting ready for work, wondering aloud why his leg felt so heavy, I would squeal with laughter and cry when he had to either pry me loose or be late for work.

My father grew up on a farm in northern Italy and told me that when he was born, he was strapped to a board so his spine would grow straight. As if being strapped down instilled him with an insatiable urge to wander, he spent his young adulthood working in the restaurants of transatlantic ships. My mother met him aboard a boat on the open sea, on her way to study in Italy when she was twenty-three. He always worked in restaurants, considered a proper profession in his culture. In American culture, being a waiter was the domain of college students and people who were in between "real jobs." This attitude affected his self-esteem. In the traditional Italian family he came from, a man provides for his family, but my mother earned more working at the Italian consulate than he did as a waiter. My mother's father was a doctor, and my father went from serving the country club crowd at a restaurant to socializing among them during his off time. He never seemed comfortable in my mother's upper-middle-class environs; my grandmother always says he was out of his element.

While he was working at an Italian restaurant, he began to shift from wine to vodka. The staff socialized after work—such was the life of a waiter in America—and he was probably more at ease around his restaurant colleagues than he was with my mother's friends. My father wasn't used to drinking hard liquor, or drinking that much of it. He started coming home later, and he and my mother started fighting. I was only three at the time, but I recall two episodes: the car accident and the sculpture incident.

I don't know whether my father hit a tree or another car, or whether anyone was hurt. I only remember him pacing in the driveway as my mother stood there watching. His white Honda had been towed back to the house, totaled. My father leaned forward and pushed back into place one of the parking lights, which now dangled from a wire. The light popped back out again.

A few months later I came home from a preschool art class with an abstract sculpture made of wire, clay, and driftwood. I proudly displayed it on my dresser. Late at night, a few nights after I brought the sculpture home, I was startled out of my sleep by the loud voices of my parents arguing. My father then came into my room, picked up my sculpture, and hurled it against the wall. It shattered everywhere, and I cowered under the covers. It was out of character for my loving father to do something purposefully destructive, especially toward me.

The following year, 1984, my mother joined the foreign service, and after a training period in Washington, D.C., she was assigned to her first post, in Guadalajara, Mexico. My father came along and stayed until my mother divorced him a year later. I was six. He returned to Seattle, to a studio apartment and his job at the Italian restaurant. When I visited him, he always seemed depressed, though he tried to wear a smile for my benefit.

I saw him during summers, from when I was six until I was seventeen. My mother wouldn't let me stay with him, saying that his work hours were too unpredictable and his neighborhood wasn't safe, so I stayed at my maternal grandmother's and visited him on his days off. Dad days were visits to the aquarium, Volunteer Park, and Urban Outfitters in the hip neighborhood where he lived. All year long I looked forward to summers in Seattle.

In my early teens I realized exactly how similar we were. We looked alike, with our olive skin and dark hair and eyes. I identified with his need for solitude, his love of getting lost in a movie and walking through the city or on the paths around Volunteer Park. We were both woolgatherers. We listened to the same music (Sonic Youth, Smashing Pumpkins, Nirvana) and always agreed on video store selections.

For a long time I blamed my mother for keeping me from my father. Drinking allowed me to forget that he wasn't present. My father's absence was not because my mother was bitter (she wasn't) but because he was an alcoholic. I'd been able to deny it to myself until then.

My first concrete memory of this realization was one Sunday during one of my summer visits with my father, the year I was sixteen. We decided to go to the beach. When I met him at his apartment building, I noticed his body swaying as we walked toward his front door to go into his apartment and pack our picnic. It was 11:00 AM and he was drunk. I put together the pieces of my life's primary puzzle: *What's wrong with my father?* His drinking was the problem.

"Why are you looking at me like that?" he asked.

"I'm not," I said. I walked to the refrigerator, pulled out a Coke, and cracked it open.

We took the bus to Madison Park, a beach on Lake Washington. After the white-car incident, he never drove. On our picnic, he tried to hide it but I saw him pour vodka into a thermos. Then he poured in juice. I stared out over Lake Washington. My father lay on his back, soaking up the sun.

At the end of the day, when my grandmother's pale blue Toyota pulled up in front of his building to pick me up, my father muttered in Italian, "*Sono finito con queste genti.*" I'm done with these people. Even though he was right in front of me, he was already gone. That day, at age sixteen, I came to a full awareness of what my father had tried to conceal.

Two years later, while in film school in Boston, I came home to find a letter I'd sent to my father returned undeliverable. I tried calling, but his phone was disconnected. I wanted to go to Seattle, but my mother convinced me to stay at school and focus on my studies. No one seemed to be trying very hard to find him, including me. Pretending everything was fine and immersing myself in my new life at college was far easier than taking time off to try to figure out where he'd gone. On some level I must have been afraid of what I might uncover, though at the time I would have said I was heeding my mother's advice.

He resurfaced right around the time I graduated, on a postcard with a picture of Portofino and a few scribbled sentences. He had moved back to Italy. Something about it didn't sit right, but at least he was there. The postmark said so. It took another four years to find out why my father had disappeared. This was the secret my family was keeping from me.

Two weeks after my twenty-fifth birthday, at the Thanksgiving table at my grandmother's house, Grandma had a thimble too many of red wine and told me there were some things about my father I didn't know but probably should. "It's been six years," she said.

"Since what?" I asked.

My grandmother put down her fork and told the story that confirmed my suspicion about why my father had returned to Italy.

My grandmother had run into a family friend, Roberto, on the street. Roberto told her he was worried; he had run into my father.

My father was living outside, Roberto said. Homeless. He had been evicted from his apartment. He had shown up drunk for work at the restaurant and then stopped showing up at all. Whether he quit or was fired, I don't know, but the family friend told my grandmother that he had found my father living in Volunteer Park—the place we used to go for long walks. My grandparents went to search the park. They found my father lying on the grass, his ankles swollen, toenails grown long, and clothing tattered.

My grandparents tried to coax him from the park, but he wouldn't go. Sometime during all this, my mother told my grandmother never to tell me about my father's becoming homeless. She wanted to protect me. After a few more tries, they succeeded in getting him off the ground and to the hospital, where he was treated for cirrhosis. They bought him a plane ticket back to Italy. My father was now in his sixties and back living with his mother. In America he'd had a reverse immigrant experience: He didn't have much, but he had lost everything.

I finished my glass of red wine that Thanksgiving eve, feeling that something had clicked into place—I was now forced to grasp the extent of my father's alcoholism and how drastic his situation had become. Yet I had a strangely calm "this is how it is" reaction to this realization, which I later learned was typical for the child of an alcoholic.

The last time I saw him, my father made a point of alluding to his sobriety. My mother and I went to Genoa and stayed with him for three days. (The two of them had remained amicable over the years.) My father fixed dinner and poured a deep orange-colored drink into three cocktail glasses. It was some combination of tropical juices.

"No alcohol," he said. "There is no alcohol here."

He hadn't told me his version of how he had ended up back in Italy, and I didn't ask. I feared that bringing it up would add too much weight to our brief time together, and I wanted us to enjoy these moments. More than that, I didn't want to cause him any shame. He looked healthy, and I was relieved.

The next day we walked by the docks and visited the city's new aquarium, strolling through darkened rooms full of fish, often in silence save for water lapping against the edges of the open tanks. I reached for my father's arm and he smiled, his teeth white and straight. The visit was short, but I saw it as the first step in a process of rebuilding. We were setting the stage for spending a longer time together in the future, maybe even an entire month. Probably August, we agreed.

August came and went unrealized, as most of our plans had been. I took my usual "disappointment is normal" approach. I was frustrated but not surprised, trying to focus again on things I could control or at least rely on: work, friendships, writing.

I heard nothing more about my father until my mother received an email from his younger brother. My father had started drinking again. He stayed inside his apartment, refusing to see anyone. I considered going there, but my mother thought it was a bad idea. Who could say what my father would do or in what kind of condition I would find him? I went back and forth with the idea of showing up on his doorstep but never had the chance to decide.

My father died on July 2, 2008. I didn't find out until a week after he was admitted, comatose, to the hospital. His younger brother had called my mother from Italy. He'd been on vacation and came back to the news that my father had died. I emailed my uncle seeking answers. "Your father is in the Christian heaven. Stay strong," he wrote back.

Now that my father was dead, I no longer had to wonder why we weren't in contact. During this time, my own drinking habits remained the same: cocktails with friends, wine at parties, and happy hour with colleagues. Usually I had two drinks. Occasionally more.

Three years later, entire weeks pass with hardly a thought of my father's death. Then it will hit me out of nowhere, while I'm unloading the dishwasher, fixing dinner, or reading a book. If I had flown to Italy and shown up on his doorstep, would he have known that somebody, his daughter, cared enough to try to stop him? Save him? What was it about the alcohol that he couldn't quit? At what point does it become too late? If I'd had the chance to ask him these questions, might I not be so consumed with my own drinking?

I read an article in *The New York Times Magazine* called "The 'Wet House' Where Alcoholics Can Keep Drinking" by Benoit Denizet-Lewis. It tells of "chronically homeless and alcoholic men," members of the "unfortunates," who will drink themselves to death. That's what my father was, a so-called unfortunate, one who couldn't quit and lost his life as a result. The story shed new light on his situation for me—that he was not alone. "I've fought it my whole life, and it has cost me my whole life," one resident is quoted as saying. Maybe this is what my father would have said if we had been able to talk about it.

It's been eleven years since my mother cautioned me at that bar in Greece. I still drink socially, only now I pay close attention, monitoring my alcohol intake in a way that lends new meaning to the expression "keeping tabs." I measure and calculate. I notice the level of liquid in my glass compared with others' glasses and sip slowly, making a point to be the last one left with a glass half full while everyone else is ordering a second round.

Will I end up an alcoholic like my dad? The answer to the question is either yes and I'm not aware of it, just as my father never seemed to be, or no. But I constantly ask myself if I might have a problem because he did. Do I drink to escape? Is it bad that I enjoy drinking a glass or two of wine when I'm alone, writing or relaxing? Is that how it started for him?

The thing about my stopping is that I don't want to. A lychee martini with Thai food, a sidecar in a bar that brings back a speak-easy vibe, a hearty glass of good pinot noir to complement pasta, a Magic Hat #9 on tap at happy hour—drinking is one of life's pleasures, and I love every drop. I pass all the online "Are you a problem drinker?" quizzes. Do you drink to get drunk? No. Black out? No. Need a drink in the morning? The idea of one makes me queasy.

Though I can't understand or change what happened to my father, I do have control over myself and, I hope, the awareness to recognize if I were losing that control. I choose to drink, despite what might lie dormant in my genes.

UNDER THE INFLUENCE

JOYCE MAYNARD

IT WAS ONE OF THOSE last warm nights of summer when you can see the first hint of red on the leaves and you know that if you haven't taken your last swim yet, you will soon. Transplanted to Northern California sixteen years earlier, I'd spent three weeks back East, visiting old friends in my home state of New Hampshire, where my adult daughter, Audrey, still lives, on the farm where I used to live, too.

Twenty-two years had passed since I had swum on the pond by our house there and read to my children on the bed I shared with their father. That chapter is closed now. But sometimes when I pass through, as I did that day, old memories catch me up short. I'm transported to the stories of the two families I was part of once—the family I made with the man I used to be married to, and the family in which I grew up, in another small town, not so far from this one.

I remember some good times. But also I remember those dark nights as the marriage was coming undone for the last time, and how—with everyone else in bed—I'd move through the rooms of our small house, laying my body down alongside first one of my sleeping children and then another, in search of sleep that would not come.

Not much of a drinker in those days—and never one to opt for the hard stuff—I took to setting my husband's Christmas bottle of Johnnie Walker Red on the kitchen counter, pouring myself a shot. Daughter of a beloved but heartbreaking alcoholic father, long dead, I recognized the dormant impulse ("When life is hard, pour a drink") as part of my legacy. That final winter of my marriage—the year I turned thirty-five—it had surfaced with alarming regularity. And because I wanted my husband to recognize my despair, and pay attention to it, I'd leave the bottle on the counter for him to see in the morning. *See what you drove me to do?* it was meant to tell him. *You've even got me drinking now.*

The marriage ended. I put away my Johnnie Walker habit, though in the years after, I discovered a fondness for wine—how it tasted and what it did to me, the dulling of the edges, the softening of the harsh aspects of my life, of which there were plenty. Two decades later, I could not name a single night I'd been drunk, but the practice of pouring myself a glass of zinfandel at day's end, to take the edge off, had become a frequent, then nightly, event. Not just one glass either. Two. Three if life seemed particularly stressful.

Now I was back in New Hampshire, my annual late-summer pilgrimage to see my daughter and my old friends and to swim in natural lakes and ponds, as opposed to the swimming pools of Marin County. It had been a wonderful trip.

That evening—our last together for a while—Audrey and I had been invited to the home of friends who own a cottage on a pond just down the road from our old place. Earlier that afternoon, we'd plunged in the water at the swimming hole we used to go to when she was little, and she'd given me a tomato from her garden. The next morning I'd be turning in my rental car and flying back out West. I was ready to be home, but I also felt the tug of leaving my daughter and a little ragged, too, as I always get from the memories dislodged by my visit back to this place.

So the glass of chianti our hosts poured for me as I stepped through the door of their cottage felt particularly welcome. Having spent the first eighteen years of my life as the daughter of a man who got drunk every night—and got up every morning to pretend it never happened—I recognized a long time ago that though I remain careful to keep my own alcohol consumption in check, the urge to reach for wine is always there when I feel sorrow or worry or simply when I'm tired. That night I was happy—feeling lucky to be with Audrey, to be with these friends, to hear the crickets outside and look out to the pond beyond their screened-in porch—but I was in a state of high emotion, too. For me, a glass of wine—and then another—served as a way of heightening my pleasure in what was feeling good around me. And dulling the rest.

Our friends are Italian American, and they had made eggplant parmigiana, along with spaghetti in a homemade sauce. There was garlic bread and fresh corn on the cob, picked that afternoon. I ate well and reached for seconds.

As for the wine, I couldn't say how much I drank because every time my glass got a little low, our host topped it off. No tipsiness evident, I could tell my friends a story or take in the details of the spaghetti sauce recipe just fine, and I even rattled off a recipe of my own for our friends. Mostly it seemed the wine had the effect of intensifying the warm glow of what would have been a wonderful evening regardless.

We left the cottage sometime around ten o'clock. My daughter's boyfriend drove us back to the cabin they share on the very piece of land where Audrey was born and where her father still lives—my old writing cabin. I said goodbye, then took out the keys for my rental car to make the twenty-minute drive to the home of a different friend, where I was staying a few towns over. Audrey had invited me to spend the night on her couch, but knowing I'd be flying out the next day, I wanted to wake up with my suitcases nearby to get my gear organized for the trip.

Four miles down the familiar dirt road I spotted it: the flashing blue light in my rearview mirror.

This stretch of road was more than familiar to me. I used to drive it every day, bringing my three children to school. On one memorable night—winter this time, a good twenty-five years earlier—my son

Charlie had dropped a tiny golden sword from his Playmobil pirate ship out the window of our station wagon at just this spot, and because I knew how much that sword meant to him, I had spent the better part of an hour circling this particular stretch of road with my high beams on, trying to locate that sword. Classic adult-child-of-alcoholic behavior there: the compulsion to protect one's child from loss and grief, not simply because the pain would be hard for him to endure but because the pain would be too hard for his endlessly vigilant and caretaking mother.

I'd found the sword. My high beams had picked up the glint on the dark highway, and I had pulled over. I was very nearly sideswiped by an eighteen-wheeler when I got out of my car and crossed the highway to retrieve it. But that night at least, I'd averted what would have felt like—to me more than to my son, probably—a heartbreak.

Now a different kind of trouble and danger had me in its grip. The speeding ticket was a certainty. But the question the officer had for me when I rolled down my window and handed him my license was, "How much have you had to drink tonight?" And the truth was, I didn't know.

"One glass of wine," I told him.

"I'm going to ask you to take a Breathalyzer test," he said.

"Do I have to?" I said. Already, here was a humiliating realization: that I might rely on some unknown legal technicality to get out of a test, based on my uncertainty about whether I could pass it.

Legally, no, I wasn't obligated to breathe into the machine, the officer told me. But now he was asking me to step outside the car and perform a few simple tests.

I stood by the side of the road, in the light of the police car, with the occasional car whizzing past, and walked a straight line, heel to toe. I stood on one leg, raising my other a few inches off the ground. For the final test, the officer moved his forefinger back and forth in front of my face and asked me to follow it without moving my head. Only my eyes.

When I was done with that one, he shook his head. "I'm placing you under arrest," he said. "Since you've been cooperative up to this point, you can wear the handcuffs in front of you rather than behind."

No need to say the kinds of thoughts and feelings that went through my brain at this moment. Horror for sure. Shame. Also fear. Regret. More shame.

A picture came to me then, of a night long before, when—with my mother out of town and my sister off at college—I had been left alone in the care of my father, who'd gone on a bender. It must have been ten o'clock when I arose to knocking on the door and the sight of a police officer.

"Do you know who the driver might be of the vehicle left in the middle of the street?" he asked. It was our family Oldsmobile. Our father must have driven most of the way home before abandoning it. With the motor still running.

In today's world, my father would have been charged with a DUI. But this was 1966. The officer, hearing the car was ours and that my father was asleep upstairs, had moved the car himself and left it in our driveway, where my father found it the next morning, likely with no memory of what had happened the night before. "Tell your dad to be more careful" was all the officer had said to me. I kept that shameful message to my twelve-year-old self.

Now here I was, by the side of another dark New Hampshire road, with no similar appearance of leniency awaiting me. Now the police officer was opening the car door for me, since my hands were locked together. Now we were heading to the police station in the town where I'd raised my children, back when they and I were young.

The police officer had arranged to have my rental car towed to a local auto repair shop—a place I knew well from a few dozen visits over the years back when I lived in this town and drove old cars, always in need of some repair or another. As for me, I sat with my handcuffs in my lap in the back seat of the cruiser as the police officer drove us along the familiar roads toward town. There was a Red Sox game on the radio. In my chest, I could feel the pounding of my heart.

At the station, they sat me in a room and explained my options. If I refused the Breathalyzer, I'd be automatically detained. If I passed the Breathalyzer, I'd be let off with only the speeding ticket. If I failed, I'd be charged with a DUI and released on bail in the custody of whomever I might find to pick me up. This would be my daughter, no doubt now asleep back at the cabin on our old farm. It was close to midnight by then.

Another fact to absorb: While the legal definition of intoxication stood, nationally, at .08 percent, in New Hampshire the police possessed discretionary power to charge an individual with driving under the influence for an alcohol level at .04 percent and above.

I had no choice now but to submit to the Breathalyzer test. The officer positioned me on a bench for a waiting time of twenty minutes. This was to make sure my test results would not be skewed by the insertion in my mouth of any foreign substance. Evidently people suspected of driving drunk and awaiting the test sometimes surreptitiously pop in a breath mint, and doing so invalidates the test results. If I even touched my mouth during the waiting period, we'd have to restart the twenty-minute wait to take the test.

"I have to keep my eyes on your mouth for twenty minutes to make sure you don't touch it or insert any mints," the officer said. He demonstrated how I could scratch my nose, if I needed to, without obstructing the sight lines to my mouth. This involved raising my arm over my head and dropping my hand over the top of my face rather than blocking my lips.

"Some people touch their face on purpose to buy more time," the officer said. "Try that two times, and it's an automatic DUI."

Still unsure how much I'd had to drink, and running through my brain all the ways my life would be altered if I lost my license, I had already considered this very idea. This was how low I had stooped,

I reflected, how desperate I felt at the prospect of what a DUI would mean to my life. Not just the inconvenience of losing my license for a period of months or the ongoing expense of high insurance. More so the shame—an emotion I remembered well from childhood, when my greatest terror lay in the prospect of someone (my friends, my teacher, our neighbors) finding out that my father got drunk.

More time passed. I thought about the eggplant parmigiana I'd eaten, grateful I'd taken those second helpings. I imagined the call to my daughter from the police, informing her that her mother was at the station, under arrest. "My daughter is a sound sleeper," I told the officer. "She might not hear the phone." Not that her picking it up.to receive his call would be good news. Shame again over the prospect of her hearing that her mother had been charged with drunk driving, as my father never had been, though he could have been, a hundred times over.

"We can send an officer out to the house to get her," he said. I pictured that scene then: Audrey waking to the sound of knocking at the door and coming downstairs to find a man in a police uniform standing there. I know what I'd think.

Twenty minutes passed; time to take the test. "Some people don't blow full force," the officer told me. "But the machine picks that up."

I took the tube in my mouth. Blew hard. Waited. Blew again. Returned to the bench.

A few minutes later a printout scrolled from the machine, like a fax: my Breathalyzer score. The officer ripped it from the machine and studied it. I said another prayer. *Just let me be okay, and I'll never let this happen again.*

He studied the paper. He disappeared into another room. Through the door I could hear the Red Sox game. A late inning now. They must be somewhere on the West Coast.

An excruciating number of minutes passed. Finally the police officer emerged. Maybe the Red Sox game was over. Maybe he just figured I'd suffered enough.

"You blew a .02," he said. "You're free to go."

Meaning an officer would drive me to the body shop where my car had been towed, the body shop of our old friend Gene. There'd be a bill for that one, too, of course, along with the $200 speeding ticket. But I knew I was lucky.

I made it back to my friend's house sometime around 1:00 AM. He'd waited up for me a while, then gone to bed. The next morning I told him the story, making it sound funny more than terrifying.

I turned in my rental car and headed to the airport, where I called Audrey to tell her what had happened. I didn't want my daughter to make the mistakes I'd made. I wanted to protect her. If I carry the legacy of potential alcohol addiction, so does she.

It was close to midnight when I arrived home in California. At that moment, I took in the full weight of what had happened the night before—how close I'd come to getting charged with a DUI and how much my life would have been changed if I'd gotten one. Not just because I live on a mountain, where every trip to buy groceries or visit the gym requires a car. But more so for the accompanying truth that, thirty years since my father's death, I had allowed myself to become addicted to the same thing that had killed him: I had to have a drink.

The fact that I had been driving under the legal limit that night offered little reassurance here. What did it matter that I wasn't drunk if the drinking had loosened my guard and dulled my judgment sufficiently that I was driving fifty-five miles per hour in a zone marked thirty? What if I was simply a poor driver, particularly shaky at night? All the more reason why my drinking that night—any amount—was a bad idea.

My daughter and my friend, hearing the story of my encounter with the police that night, had expressed indignation at the police officer. But I couldn't feel offended by his behavior—the handcuffs, the humiliating instructions for how to scratch my nose, the long wait during the ball game to hear my test results. If the officer's placing those handcuffs on me was undertaken in an effort to shake me up, he had accomplished that.

It was almost twenty-four hours later, walking in the door of my house in California after my long journey home, that I took in the full weight of what had happened the night before. Home in my own kitchen at last, I felt a powerful urge to do the thing I always want to do when I'm tired, or lonely, or scared, or simply sad: I wanted to pour myself a drink.

I went to bed instead.

SLAKE

SAMANTHA DUNN

MOM DRANK TOO MUCH.

I don't mean she got tipsy on one too many martinis at the country club. I don't mean she downed a few extra glasses of merlot while cooking meatballs in the kitchen. What I mean is that she poured the kind of scotch that comes in plastic gallon bottles into an iced-tea tumbler. She took the iced-tea tumbler to her thin lips and drank in gulps, as if it contained water and she had been trekking the Sahara. The contracting muscles of her neck always reminded me of the way a snake moves, and it seemed she had to have scales lining the inside of her throat. She never coughed or sputtered, never grimaced at the raw burn of all that ethanol. (Later, after she retired and money was tighter than usual, she drank $1.99 white zinfandel from Walmart the same way, sometimes adding Splenda to sweeten it.)

She drank like that every day I remember, every day from five o'clock until she was so drunk that her green eyes filmed over fish-like, as if she were looking up at the world from under a great sea. At some point she would stand up, sway slightly, and announce, "Time for beddy-bye!" in a singsongy voice that was so at odds with the deep ring of the way she said every other thing. The fall of her feet down the hall was a thudding, concrete, heel-first series of strikes. Never that I saw did she suffer a hangover.

"Old age should burn and rave at close of day." Mom would often quote Dylan Thomas with a wave of her cigarette, and it was also true that she recited from memory vast passages from Shakespeare, Thoreau, and Rudyard Kipling. She knew what to do with a socket wrench, spoke passable Arabic and Spanish, and tied knots in maraschino cherry stems with her tongue. She remembered all the elements of the periodic table, did long division in her head, had been an Arthur Murray dance instructor with a specialty in the rumba. Mom told jokes with the same deadpan delivery as Denis Leary, but did it even funnier, raising her right eyebrow independent of the left.

And even if she drank too much, she was a crackerjack emergency room and operating room nurse who knew how to deliver babies. In fact, so often did she cover for a golf-loving ob-gyn who never answered his pager that if you were born in a certain hospital out West in 1971 and you are a girl, odds are, your grateful parents named you Deanne after the woman who brought you into this world.

Yet when anyone who knew her describes her, they'll say she drank too much. Maybe, if they are being nice or if they didn't know her well, it won't be the first thing on their list, but eventually they'll bring it up. Trust me. I've spent a lifetime listening to people trying to break the news to me. "I know," I tell them. Or even, "Thanks for the news flash." Or sometimes, "Like you think *I* don't fucking know?"

The fact that her drinking could outweigh the absolutely magnificent brilliance of her mind and her encyclopedic knowledge and her nuclear-powered charm should be proof of its magnitude. I could talk about all the damage her drinking caused me but mostly caused her—all the ruined relationships, the firings, the evictions, the wrecked cars, the cuts and bruises, the money squandered—but now, in the months after she's dead, these are not the things that occupy my mind. What does occupy my thoughts, what has taken up residence in my head and rattles my skull late into the night, is the wondering: What, really, was she thirsting for, and how could it have been slaked?

IT HAD SOMETHING TO do with the Irish.

That's the first word Mom would use to describe herself. If pressed, she would say "gorgeous" or "brilliant" and give you a wink. Maybe next she would say "nurse" or, most likely, "Sam's mom."

"Mom, that's two words. The exercise is to describe yourself in one word."

"Well, that's a stupid exercise. Where's the fun in that?" She'd shake her head. "You, my dear, are a killjoy—anybody ever tell you that?"

Being Irish was a big part of her story. She did in fact look like she'd been sent over from central casting: wavy auburn hair, green eyes, an upturned nose, lightly freckled skin. Her beauty idol was Maureen O'Hara, but she looked more Shirley MacLaine as she got older. But her mannerisms, her way of talking and walking, the way she dressed as a young woman—those were all so startlingly similar to the way Stockard Channing played the character Rizzo in the movie version of *Grease* that now I find myself watching that musical over and over. We never took home videos.

She was Catholic, in all the deepest ways. Even when it wasn't Saint Patrick's Day, she wore ridiculous T-shirts that said WHEN IRISH EYES ARE SMILING, THEY'RE UP TO SOMETHING. She would crack you upside the head first and ask questions later—which is to say, she had a streak of the prizefighter in her. Tommy Makem and the Clancy Brothers blared from our turntable on booze-soaked Sunday afternoons. A shillelagh leaned in the corner by the front door of every home we ever lived in—I kid you not. At any moment a weird-faced dancing leprechaun could materialize in the center of our living room.

Okay, so there I exaggerate, but that kind of blarney is part of the package.

But here's the thing: None of my other relatives on her side of the family consider themselves so Irish. Our heritage does indeed include Ireland, but also Wales, Scotland, and England. There's talk of a Dutchman in there somewhere, a German down the line, and rumors of a great-great-great grandmother named Polly from the Seneca tribe. To hear Mom tell it, though, you'd think we'd all just stepped off a boat from County Clare.

This identification with all things Irish came, in part, from her having spent the long afternoons and weekends of her childhood in the company of my great-aunt and great-uncle Ethel and Jim O'Brien. My grandmother—the one single, good-looking divorcée in a small town—had cocktails with friends or went to New York City on trips for the town's one department store, where she was the lingerie buyer.

Uncle Jim indeed had come straight from Dublin, landed in Boston, and somehow ended up married to a local girl in Warren, right on the New York–Pennsylvania state line. Uncle Jim must have been for my mom the practical father, the man who did all the things her own father didn't do after he left to start another family in another town.

But that isn't everything about why Mom felt so Irish. I wonder now what it was like for her to be a forgotten only child, sitting in that careful house with two aging relatives, lace doilies on the furniture and a framed picture of the pope staring down from the wall. Did the thirst start there? Maybe it began as a dry scratch in the back of her throat. Likely she confused it with hunger at first; many old black-and-whites from those years show a rotund little girl smiling from behind a table loaded with plates of potatoes and roasts, a stern-jawed Aunt Ethel in an assortment of floral-patterned aprons standing in the kitchen.

Did Mom listen to Uncle Jim talk as he nursed his Jameson, telling tales about the emerald place he'd left in that sentimental, morose way of the immigrant idealizing the motherland, and did the deepest part of her resonate with the feeling of exile? Exile if not from a place then from the mother and the father for whom she longed.

"Oh, for the love of Christ, what bullshit," she'd say to that. I can see her rolling her eyes. "You're prone to the airy-fairy, too precious for your own good." She blamed it on my father's inferior Italian genes, the Italian love of opera and of crying at weddings and funerals.

So another theory: The whole Irish thing put a convenient label on her thirst, a reason. Say "Irish," and there was no need for further analysis. She was, after all, a woman who believed any emotional expression worth having could be conveyed with a Hallmark Shoebox greeting card. Whenever she was accused of alcoholism—by me, her mother, her boyfriends, her friends, her bosses—her reply (indignant) was that she merely drank "like an Irish person." I once heard someone say that line in a movie, and I thought, *Hey, they stole that from my mom.*

Mom had her first drink at the age of fourteen, a cocktail called a Pink Lady (gin, grenadine, light cream; any kid raised like I was has the equivalent of a bartending-school education by age six). I have a picture of the portentous occasion around here somewhere; it was snapped at a touristy bar in Manhattan in 1952. Mom, face shiny, baby fat straining the seams of her nice dress, sits next to my exquisite grandmother, who looks like a movie star in a pillbox hat and Mona Lisa red lips. Gram looks like she should be accompanied by Rock Hudson, but instead it is just some dumpy Irish guy named Patrick with a bit of a gut and a wife and five kids back in Pennsylvania. Who takes her teenage daughter on a date with a married man she's having an affair with and also buys her a drink? Gram, that's who.

I wonder if Mom was sizing him up, if she was imagining this Patrick walking through the door after work every night, smiling at the sight of her, saying, "How was your day at school, *macushla?*" I see her eyeing him and putting that Pink Lady to her lips, the grenadine sweetness and the gin burn mixing with the desire for something she did not have, conflicted feelings fusing in that moment, alcohol and wanting now confounded in the pathways of her brain for the rest of her natural life. Then again, maybe she'd been feeling awkward and uptight sitting there with her mother and old Patrick (didn't she go to school with his kids?), but the second the gin hit her system, all tension melted, the moments becoming somehow manageable. Maybe even pleasant.

Or not. Maybe she just thought the Pink Lady tasted yummy.

OF COURSE, DRINKING KILLED HER. (That sentence would piss her off to no end. She would tell you that medical incompetence killed her, that doctors are "about as useful as tits on a boar pig," and that she would still be around if I hadn't shanghaied her into the hospital. But being that I'm the one who's still alive, I get to tell the story.)

The byzantine epic of her death goes something like this: broke a glass in her kitchen; stepped barefoot on a shard; tried to treat the cut at home; it became infected; her foot went gangrenous, and half of it had to be amputated; many threatening, possibly terminal health issues were uncovered; emergency surgeries of all manner were required; a two-month hospital stay ensued; while she was recovering, a secondary infection attacked; she went septic; rushed to the hospital again; died after two weeks. (To tell you the details requires more fortitude and bravery than I possess right now.)

Still, the thirst.

A little story to illustrate: She returns to our home after having been in the hospital for two months. She hobbles up the steps—half her foot amputated—and goes straight into the kitchen. I'm in the living room with my son when I hear her rummaging around in the cupboard.

"Mom, what are you looking for?"

"Where the hell's the vodka you had in here?"

The next day, when the ambulance came, she'd downed more than half a liter of booze. The thing is, I knew she'd do that. I knew it from a lifetime. Yet I still cried.

I want to be clear here: I know about drinking. I have a veritable black belt in Al-Anon. I have researched addiction for books I have written, interviewed Dr. Drew (the "rehab doctor" on television) more than once for articles in *O, The Oprah Magazine,* blah blah blah blah blah. Disease, genetic predisposition, environment, psychological factors—yes, yes, I know. I know it all, and yet none of it seems enough to explain that quenchless thing of my mother's. Maybe biology, psychology, sociology, and whatever other -ologies we invent can explain and contain the addictions suffered by some. For others, the immensity dwarfs our science.

It is a mystery. Many things are.

Somehow I got the idea early that maybe if I were successful enough, I could kill this quenchless thing. But of course not. I hoped—hoped in secret, because I knew better by then—that the birth of my son, Mom's beloved grandson, would finally make the thing evaporate. Even that, no. Over the course of my life I have raged at this thing and run away from this thing, I have screamed at this thing and beat up this thing, I have tried to intellectualize, and ultimately to accept, this thing. Now, after it and she are gone, what I have come to feel is a strange sort of objective curiosity, perhaps even a bizarre kind of reverence.

Final picture: Mom, bloated body in a hospital bed, hooked up to all manner of tubes, her system shutting down. Doctors have restricted liquids for fear that she'll aspirate and get pneumonia, or choke to death, or some other horror I don't understand. The only thing they've okayed are these green sponge lollipops. I soak them in my bottled water and hand them to her to suck on when she's conscious enough to want one.

Now she motions me closer with a wave of her finger.

"Honey, I want some Coke."

Her whisper is dry, a croak, but it is still the voice of my mom. And although the words that first form on my lips are *No, the doctors say no,* I let them dissolve before they reach air. What's the point? I don't want to be the person who says the thing that should be said. I just want to be her daughter, so I tell her, "Be right back," and I run and get the contraband from the cafeteria downstairs.

Her eyes are shut when I return, and the machines seem too quiet. For an ugly moment I think I'm too late. But then her breath shudders and she wakes up to see me. I hold the Coke up to her bed.

See, I got it.

Goody goody.

The sodium carbonate in the sponge lollipop makes the Coke fizz even more. It takes just a second to saturate. As I bring it close to her lips, she lays her hand over mine to guide me, her skin unbelievably smooth, almost silken. Her leathery mouth gapes eagerly when she takes the lollipop in.

She shuts her eyes and I see her swallow, then grimace. She coughs harshly. I bring a tissue to her mouth and wonder, *What have I done?*

Are you okay?

She nods slightly and gives me a wink.

Yummy.

More?

I expect she will say yes—because really, when has she ever said no?—and I start to douse another sponge lollipop. But then I see her move her head side to side. "No, honey."

Enough? Did that hit the spot?

Hit the spot.

I put my hands over hers. We stay like that for I don't know how long. In the early hours of the next morning, she will be dead.

WHAT'S THE BIG DEAL?
LESSONS FOR SCHOOLCHILDREN AND THEIR PARENTS

LAURA JOFRE

RECENTLY I HEARD THE PHRASE "drunk parents" pass between my two older kids, ages eleven and fourteen. *Could they be talking about my husband and me?*

We were sitting nearby in the kitchen, simply sharing a late dinner with a glass of wine. But our kids, successfully indoctrinated by their fifth-grade Drug Abuse Resistance Education (DARE) program, now believe that *all* drinking is bad.

Thanks to the DARE program, Sofie and Luca are well informed about alcohol, as well as drug pushers and peer pressure. They are prepared to deal with cyberbullies, smokers, and strangers, not to mention classmates who bring vodka to lunch. (This actually happened in my daughter's middle school. Her reaction: "Didn't that girl go to DARE? I thought drinking was *bad.*")

I am grateful to the DARE program for teaching them frankly about subjects that are so fraught. But I am not grateful that the wine my husband and I enjoy with dinner now feels like a crime. How did this happen? DARE notwithstanding, I had always intended to raise my kids with a moderate attitude that would culminate in the whole family's enjoying some wine at the dinner table, even if all members were not quite twenty-one.

Maybe this was magical thinking. I didn't know how kids' brains worked when I made that plan; I wouldn't find out until I was in the thick of the Drinking Issue. I'd forgotten my own teen years, when I interpreted the no-drinking rule to mean "Don't get caught." I heeded the "This is your brain on drugs" message and stayed off drugs, but I didn't internalize any public health warnings about drinking. There were drunk-driving accidents and other terrible consequences in my own school community, but like so many teenagers, I felt immortal and craved the exciting and the forbidden. It wasn't until I was in college, on a junior semester in Spain, that my relationship with alcohol progressed at all.

I don't know what the Spanish drinking age was—if there was one—but I do know that the college cafeteria sold beer and wine, which students and teachers casually sipped with their meals. It was a twilight zone in which the tension of illicit underage drinking was absent. Some of my fellow American students panicked in their new freedom and, much to the amusement or disdain of our Spanish peers, ordered two or three beers at a time.

I, meanwhile, lounged with a glass of red wine and a volume of Nabokov, trying to impress a brooding Spanish intellectual without revealing my halting Spanish-class Spanish. I soon discovered that, just as a martini contains a juicy and alcoholic olive, a glass of *vino tinto* contains a pearl of Spanish fluency. A glass of red wine diminished my verb conjugation anxiety and allowed me into the conversation. And conversation, connection, and discovery were what drinking with Spaniards was all about.

I continued to travel postcollege with my husband, Jaime, and saw again and again how drinking was able to leap cultural divides and produce wonderful moments of synchronicity. It's been over twenty years, but I still remember discussing World Cup soccer with German tourists at the next table. I recall sampling sherry with a proud Andalusian waiter and mulled wine with a comical Austrian bartender.

I also remember seeing families dining out with a bottle of wine on the table. Before we had children, Jaime and I noted this practice often as we stopped for a beer in a plaza or a glass of wine in a café.

I can still picture a multigenerational family sitting around a shaded table crowded with food and bottles. A boy at the table gripped his water glass with two hands, while two other kids fluttered nearby. A gray-haired man wearing a sports jacket gestured grandly, his diminutive wineglass making his hand seem large. I sensed a calm, congenial, normalcy that suggested to me, *This is European family life*. It was one family on one day, but I went ahead and made that part stand for the whole.

It may be a fantasy of sweeping simplification, but while I was traveling around Europe and eventually living there, I developed an impression of European life. It embraces more than a few stereotypes: Europeans enjoy life's pleasures where Americans ascribe danger. Europeans take what they please from life where Americans are black-and-white, not to mention judgmental. Europeans don't have positions like "I don't eat meat" or "I don't drink" and can sip the occasional aperitif without having an identity crisis about it. It's a question of moderation, of practicality; it's the question "What's the big deal?"

Drinking was a very big deal to my first obstetrician, in New York City. She was bossy and prescribed bossy books. One of her rules was No Drinking. Also No Sweets. At All. So I was grimly, dutifully, self-righteously abstaining. I missed the cocktails and cookies, but I admit I found the unconditional rule easy to follow and gratifying.

When I was six months pregnant, Jaime and I moved from New York to London for his job. I was glad to explore someplace new, though disappointed to forgo a pint in a pub to enhance the experience. My new English doctor, Mrs. L. (yes, in England she was referred to as Mrs. instead of Dr.), was amused at this notion of complete abstention and immediately recognized the "all or nothing" attitude as American. I hadn't thought of myself that way—hadn't I always admired those relaxed Europeans?—but I turned out to be a product of my country. Mrs. L., so reasonable and realistic, said, "An occasional glass of wine won't be a problem." And she said I could have a piece of cake. And she sent me to a prenatal class, where her lesson in European moderation was reinforced: The English ladies all agreed with our instructor that a glass of wine was fine. The other Americans in the class exchanged glances. I kept my head down, like Switzerland, and hid my smile.

When Sofie was born, the London hospital served Jaime and me a champagne dinner, but I couldn't drink. It tasted wrong, and I had shifted my worry from prenatal development to postnatal alcohol poisoning. A nurse recommended drinking the occasional pint of Guinness to promote my breast milk. "It's the yeast," she said knowingly. It sounded like an old wives' tale, appealing and probable, like brandy cures colds. But I didn't do it; I was afraid of tainting Sofie.

After a few months, Mrs. L. encouraged me to find a sitter. She agreed with my nurse about the health benefits of Guinness, and, more important, she was certain that regaining my adult social life and a sense of balance would prevent my suffocating under the weight of new motherhood. She convinced me that Sofie would not suffer from the trace amounts of alcohol spiking my breast milk from a glass of wine.

A prenatal-class friend, Sarah, invited Jaime and me to lunch and to dinner, introducing us to London social drinking customs: Sunday roast lunch with the family needs a glass of wine. Seven in the evening needs a glass of champagne. A pub lunch needs a beer while the kids play in the garden-cum-playground out back. I marveled at this setup and also at the fact that, although the drinking age is eighteen, parents can order a beer for their sixteen- or seventeen-year-old if it is with a meal.

Sarah also found us a mother-and-baby group that met at a member's house for lunch. Wine was sometimes offered, and no one raised an eyebrow if I did or did not drink. No one cared. It was more shocking to my English friends if I refused a cup of tea in the afternoon. While we bonded over our new-mother concerns, I always felt like a foreigner. Until one night at the pub, when once again drinking was a force for good.

The mothers took me to the Ladbroke Arms. I was about to order that pint of Guinness but was told it was too manly, too serious—they didn't care if it was good for my breast milk. They explained their drink of choice that evening: the shandy. Lager and lemonade. Yes, my American stomach clenched at that recipe, but "lemonade" in England is lemon soda, so it became less disgusting and more funny. I enjoyed the drink but could stomach only one, because it didn't really taste that good. I remember the faces of my girlfriends: mocking my ignorance, laughing at my reaction, confident in my approval, and, finally, appreciative of the unity and intimacy that come from everyone drinking the same thing, together. After months of lonely expatriate pregnancy and new-mother stress, all I needed to recalibrate was a drink in a pub with friends.

Back home in New York, living in the suburbs, it's been harder to relax and connect the same way. I'm not studying abroad, on vacation, or on an expat assignment. My town doesn't have plazas and beer gardens; it has schools and sports fields. Parents gather on the sidelines, at school events, at the farmers' market, in the park—where there is no café. This well-off community, whose children are at such great risk from drunk driving and alcohol abuse, this community that pays for the DARE program to be taught to ten-year-olds, is not as openly appreciative of the good a drink can do. I find myself defensive of the age-old equation: Good wine equals good cheer. The idea of a pub with a playground in the back is ridiculous here. I know parents who won't even drink in front of their kids; they don't want to set the wrong example.

Sarah tells me that alcohol is also a daunting problem among English teens, and of course adults, too. Alcoholism is widespread. So the "moderate" European society doesn't produce universally moderate teens. Still, Sarah believes in educating her kids about alcohol and at some point sharing a glass of wine with them around the table. Otherwise, she believes, complete denial would lead to complete excess.

I have three kids now, and I know that whatever is denied them—a puppy, a trampoline—becomes extra alluring. Luckily, I have not had any teenage alcohol disasters in my family, but Sofie, now fourteen, has seen the ominous DARE warnings materialize among her peers: the lying, the sneaking, the lawbreaking, and the terrifying overindulgence that leaves disastrous social consequences (or leaves by ambulance, in the case of the kid with vodka in the lunchroom).

As I've watched this happen, I've done my own forbidding and offered Sofie unlimited rides home. I've told the kids I'm allowed to drink because I'm a grown-up, with a fully developed body and mind. But at the same time, part of me—the European traveling part—agrees with Sarah and still harbors that intention of instilling a moderate attitude among my clan. I'm not about to hand a beer to my eleven-year-old, but I came up with a plan that I thought would be appropriate.

At one of our recent Shabbat dinners, I served the kids a sip of wine in the beautiful antique glasses my mother had passed on to us. There was a fair amount of giggling and balking and very little appreciation for the fruit of the vine. The next week I did it again, and they all refused it, saying it was wrong for them to drink wine. Maybe that was the moment, uncomfortable though it was, when the middle ground could have been explored—a perfect example of drinking alcohol not to get drunk but to appreciate, together at a family meal, the ritual of wine drinking as well as the bounty we had before us. But I froze. I suddenly saw myself not as guiding them to a future life of moderation but as teaching them to drink now. To find myself thinking, *Come on, it's just a sip* was alarming; the kids would have whipped out their DARE whistles. Just as my bossy obstetrician had advised, absolutes are easy and comforting. The week after that, I poured them apple juice: same ritual, different fruit, no middle ground.

I figured Jaime and I would just continue to have our own glasses of wine and leave the kids out of it, but then I heard that phrase, "drunk parents." The kids still chafe at the bottle of wine on the table. Drinking is bad. Can I explain to Sofie that drinking vodka at lunch *is* bad but that in a few years drinking a glass of wine in good company will melt her inhibitions and allow her to bond with foreign people and places, as Mom did in her Spanish heyday? I can't, really. I can't compare my late-college experiences to her early teenage ones. She's not ready, and that's why she shouldn't drink, not yet.

Teenagers don't readily recognize moderation. They, more than anyone else, binge, overwork, slack off, or make absolutist announcements like "I'm never eating meat again" and "Drinking is bad." One day Sofie will grow out of this teenage brain.

I suspect my kids will not be dry until their twenty-first birthdays, when they will suddenly go to a lovely café and sip a glass of chardonnay. But for me, it's about showing them a life where alcohol is not a demon but an asset and helping them arrive there safely. I look forward to the day when I can share not only a meal but also a bottle of wine with my children. I might have to spring for a trip to Europe in the process.

PART 5 REVELATIONS

TOO MUCH IS BARELY ENOUGH

"If you resolve to give up smoking, drinking, and loving,
you don't actually live longer; it just seems longer."

—Clement Freud

HALF PAST SIX

KATHRYN HARRISON

I NEVER DRANK AS A TEENAGER, and I drank infrequently in college and graduate school. It wasn't until I was thirty and had quit my day job to work full-time at home that I began to appreciate the effects of alcohol and discovered I could drink most of my friends under the table. After a night of dissipation, I bounded out of bed bright eyed, bushy tailed, and highly irritating to my hungover friends. A gift, I thought, especially for an introvert who likes going to the occasional party.

Alcohol dissolves my anxiety about meeting people and making conversation. After a couple of martinis, the prospect of socializing goes from a painful test I'm afraid I'm going to fail to something I know I'll enjoy. Alcohol loosens and sharpens my tongue, fuels ill-advised conversations and the kind of fleeting and delicious flirtations available even to those of us who have been faithfully bonded for a quarter of a century. It dismantles the defensive carapace behind which I tend to hide, not intentionally but as a reflex. A cool, seamless, and apparently indifferent facade, it once inspired a new colleague to refer to me behind my back as the ice queen. He told me so himself when we were laughing over drinks at an office Christmas party. "I wish you could have seen yourself when you walked in for that interview," he said, shaking his head. "You're nothing like the way you first appear."

I had fun at that party—it had an open bar—but I went home chastened. "Yes," my new husband said, "you can come off that way," my reserve mistaken for arrogance. We embarked on training me to smile and to offer my hand with what looked like enthusiasm. "It's not that you're unfriendly," he said, "not underneath. I know how much fun you can be. But, sweetheart, how will anyone else know if you don't look at people's faces when you meet them and don't even try to talk to them?"

The lessons, the practicing—they didn't work. But alcohol—alcohol was an elixir, a potion. Alcohol was the catalyst required for what would become a favorite diversion, providing me the means to collect fodder for party postmortems, which, truth to tell, my husband and I often enjoy more than the parties themselves.

"Come on," one of us will say in response to the other's threatening to duck an invitation to the kind of function we attend less as a couple than as separate collectors of impressions to share later, in the cab or over breakfast. "Think about who else is coming. Think about tomorrow."

If, as when I was pregnant, I don't allow myself to drink, I avoid situations that make me feel as I did when I was ten or fifteen: awkward, tongue-tied, and looking frantically for an opportunity to bolt. *How do they do it?* I'd marvel as I watched my children pass through adolescence willing, even eager, to navigate adolescent social gatherings, memories of which retain the ability to make me cringe. Until I had children of my own to observe, I didn't understand how shy—antisocial—I'd been as a teenager, and I find myself looking back on that girl with a compassion I never felt for her at the time. I don't know that I saw beyond the image I presented to classmates I never met outside of school: a studious girl who found it easier to talk to teachers than to fellow students, who passed through locker rooms and hallways with her eyes cast down and her face hidden behind her hair. She studied through every weekend, the girl I was, and for many years starved herself as though the goal were to disappear entirely. It was a late epiphany in my case: *So this is why there are bars at parties.* For me there is no celebration—and nothing to celebrate—without the amalgam of anesthesia and disinhibition that alcohol delivers, and I look for the bar first, even before I scan the crowd for a familiar face. But that's about my life out in the world, different from my life at home.

It's been twenty years now that I've made a living in the same physical environment in which I sleep and wake, in which I cook and eat and wash dishes and clothes. For all those years, the one reliable means of ending a workday has been alcohol. Although I can't leave work, alcohol provides me passage not to a different home but to one revealed in a different light and mood. It allows me to leave my working self behind, abandon her in a previous mode of being. Uncorking a bottle of wine means I've stopped writing—struggling, striving—to spend time with my family and to catch up on chores I refuse to acknowledge during hours set aside for work. I've tried to come up with a substitute—going for a run, say, or to a yoga class, but I'm a mother. I have to be home at the very moment I want to leave. So I pour a glass of wine, preside over homework, assemble dinner, and listen to my younger daughter practice the viola, which sounds better—oh so very much better—to the intoxicated ear.

And there's my constitution to consider, my overachieving liver. Even when I was a college girl, one drink barely took the edge off. The years went by, I bought bigger wineglasses, and eventually two glasses weren't enough. Then, suddenly, neither were three, and martinis became something I drank at home rather than the occasional treat out at a restaurant or bar. Was it in 2008 that I began to make sure there was always a bottle of Grey Goose in the freezer? Admittedly—I admitted it—I was firmly in the habit of pouring myself a drink when I came downstairs at five. I didn't stop to consider if I wanted a drink any more than a commuter would ask herself if she wanted to board the train out of the city and back to the suburbs. More often than not, by dinner I'd had two. The old saw about martinis—that they are like breasts: Two are perfect, a third one too many—didn't apply to me. I could enjoy being a three-breasted drinker.

I like drinking; I like it a lot. Actually, I love it. I love the way it slows the world down—slows me down—insulating me from life's endless little aggravations. And with three children, three cats, a dog, a rabbit, and an untidy husband, aggravations are guaranteed, even plentiful. But there was a way to open the refrigerator, note the jar of honey lying on its side, lid unscrewed and contents oozing from one shelf down to the next and finally pooling in that unreachable spot under the vegetable drawer, and not burst into angry tears and mutinous feelings about preparing dinner. A martini in hand, I could contemplate the honey and summon, as I often do, my older daughter's wry observation at twelve (hands on hips, feet planted, and wearing a supercilious expression I'd be hard-pressed to accept graciously from an adult) that if I'd wanted peace and quiet, maybe I shouldn't have had three children. The only half-serious recrimination, delivered with my daughter's impeccable timing, retains the capacity to make me laugh as I did when I heard it the first time.

But even a woman who wanted each of her three children and discovered in them a joy she never anticipated might cry at the thought of hours of her time squandered by spilled honey. Inevitably, children do spill; they break things; they test-drive new Magic Markers on a freshly painted white wall; they stain the Stainmaster carpeting; they succumb, never collectively, but one by one, to the stomach flu. And the only choice a mother has is how she responds to these tribulations. A martini or two casts the necessary spell that allows me to get used to the idea of spending a punitively sticky stint on my knees before an open refrigerator. I'll wonder how long it takes for raw, no-longer-cold chicken to spoil and decide to put it off until morning and a strong-to-the-point-of-galvanic coffee.

Caffeine is a substance I control with far more attention than I do alcohol, with a respect born of heart palpitations, sweaty palms, and a feeling of suffocation, the very symptoms I'd suffer under the pressure of having to make clever conversation with a stranger. One cup in the morning, and that's it. "Meet me for coffee" is an invitation I almost always counter with, "Let's wait until five and meet for a drink." In our family, the standard response to a long face was, "What's the matter with you? You look like half past six," an adage coined by my great-grandfather to describe the disappointment of having come home from work in time for dinner but having missed the cocktail hour.

As the workday winds down, I trend in the opposite direction, wound tighter and tauter. Sitting at my desk, I once clenched my teeth so hard that I broke a molar, and the first thing I do after a first drink is luxuriate in how easily I can move my neck and shoulders. I love the gradual whole-body release of tension that alcohol kindles. Even more, I love how alcohol acts on my mind, granting me passage to latitudes of my psyche I don't visit when not under its influence.

Unlike the sober, striving me, so fixed on who she's becoming that she gives her present incarnation the merest flick of disapproving attention, I arrive—after a couple of martinis—at a state of complete, savage honesty, as if looking through a lens turned inward and trained on myself, revealing who I am, not who I want or plan to be. I even do it calmly, without judgment.

That's why I stopped drinking at the new year, not forever but for a month, which was long enough to get used to living without drinking, long enough to recalibrate my relationship with alcohol and return myself to the thirtysomething version of me, the one with the strictly enforced "no drinking two nights in a row" policy.

I didn't stop when my husband said it wasn't okay to drink three glasses of wine or two martinis every night; I didn't stop when he pointed out that some might judge my behavior that of an alcoholic; nor did I stop when he said that my sharpened wit wasn't always as funny as it was acerbic.

I stopped after I'd deliberately considered how I depended on alcohol *while* I was under its influence. Drunk, I asked myself if I was an alcoholic and answered no, I wasn't. Not yet. But I did drink three times as much as the acceptable norm for women (one drink per day and no more than seven per week, according to the National Institute on Alcohol Abuse and Alcoholism). The honest, intoxicated me considered just how much I was relying on ending my day in a state of intoxication and concluded that I might be in danger of becoming one.

It was, as I expected, not only possible to quit but relatively easy—enough that I could do it on my own, from one day to the next, without the support of a group or a therapist. There were evenings when I looked like half past six, but it didn't hurt that, as I discovered after a week of abstinence, the antidepressants on which I depend are more effective when I don't drink, infusing me with unfamiliar optimism. Too, while I'm no longer an anorexic, I retain that persona's steely willpower, as well as her aesthetic preference for lean lines over curves. A middle-aged woman can't continue to drink as I was, and keep eating, too, without gradually gaining weight, and there was no way I was going to buy jeans in a larger size.

Anorexia continues to save me from alcoholism, as it did in college, when I always chose calorie-free intoxication via drugs over the wicked empty calories of alcohol. Anorexia was something my former analyst called a maladaptation, conceived at a time when I felt angry, frightened, and powerless. Maladaptive or not, I don't consider all its aspects negative. Anorexia requires self-discipline and the ability to work tirelessly toward a goal; both attributes have served me well over the years. It's also, in my experience, as much addiction as disease, one I learned to manage the same way a dry drunk controls his or her intake of alcohol. My behavior around food has been forcibly normalized, my anorexic self fettered, as she cannot be destroyed. It took decades, but I learned how to defuse a dangerous practice and salvage its useful elements. To establish good eating habits—to eat—I needed what an alcoholic needs to abstain: willpower. And I relied on motivation I couldn't always summon on

my own behalf, the impetus inspired by the same spillers and break-
ers and viola screechers whose evening antics drew me toward the
vodka in the freezer, cold enough that my hand left its silhouette
melted into the frost on its bottle.

After all, I have a son and two daughters. I pray they never know
the misery of an eating disorder; I want them to have healthy relationships to alcohol. I can be childishly defiant when my husband
makes paternalistic pronouncements, and I didn't answer when he
asked if I wanted to be a mother who modeled drinking every evening as normal behavior. But I heard him, and I thought about what
he said, and I stopped.

I'm lucky, I know, because while I missed those glasses of wine
and inexpertly mixed martinis, it was possible to walk away from
them, just as I can smoke as many cigarettes as I like at a party without wanting one the next day; just as I was lucky when in college I
experimented with drugs without getting hooked on them. An accident of brain chemistry, perhaps, or of DNA, like the one that left
me vulnerable to anorexia. But a lucky accident—to be insulated and
perhaps saved from one addiction by the remnants of another. Otherwise, given a few more years, I might be in a church basement,
clutching a Styrofoam cup of coffee and introducing myself to my
fellow AA members, a social contretemps that for me would be tol-
erable (and fodder for postmeeting postmortems) only with a martini in my hand.

THE BABY SHOWER

LIANNE STOKES

I DIDN'T END UP A THIRTY-year-old woman who lives with her parents because I had a plan. While my friends were getting promoted at PR firms in New York City and building irrigation systems in Africa, I was drinking Miller High Life and wearing a MY PRETTY PONY T-shirt in my childhood room. Not the best timing to receive an invitation to a friend's baby shower.

"Hope to see you there. It would mean the world to Emma!" her sister had written in the lower-left-hand corner of the pink engraved card. This was clearly code for *Lianne, I know you're not doing well right now, but scrounge up what is left of your dignity and be on time.*

I had quit my job as a copywriter at an ad agency and moved home to concentrate on my career in stand-up comedy. I thought it would only be a few months before I saved money and got a new apartment, but it turned out to be a year. I had no bartending or waitress experience and was fired from a receptionist job after I accidentally hung up on the CEO's wife when she phoned to tell him she was in labor. Turns out I was a failure at being a starving artist.

Emma was my former coworker from when I worked in advertising. She was an account supervisor who color-coded her file folders and played golf. Meanwhile, I'd show up to work at 11:00 AM with a latte and then realize I'd forgotten to put on a bra. We were completely opposite yet had a bond. She was everything I wasn't:

financially responsible, hyperorganized, mature. However, it was Emma who was always front row at my stand-up shows. She loved my rebellious spirit, and I had always appreciated her kindness.

I'd met Emma's friends throughout the years and felt they always looked down on me as "Emma's crazy comedian friend." As if I were their court jester. I didn't want to spend the day at a bridal shower with these snobs, especially when I was depressed, but Emma had always been so supportive of me.

That morning, I forced myself to put on a dress. It was covered in a print of ladies drinking martinis. An off-the-shoulder number, this garment was totally baby shower inappropriate. To drive home my lack of class, I arrived at the Upper East Side location without a gift.

"Hi!" Emma said when she saw me. She looked lovely, all five-foot-nine and strawberry blond of her. You could hardly tell she was pregnant save for the supersmall basketball that protruded from her lower abdomen. "I've gained twelve pounds," she said. She was almost nine months. "The doctor says I need to eat more, but I just can't fathom it."

"This isn't a dry shower, is it?" I responded. It wasn't the first time I had used booze as a crutch when I was unhappy. Getting drunk relaxed me and silenced the constant echo in my head, telling me I didn't measure up. Pinot grigio was going to get me through this. I didn't care about the consequences.

"Of course not. The bar is over there," Emma said. I walked past her and poured myself a glass of white wine. I had just taken my first sip when one of Emma's friends approached. She, too, was a natural blond, and she was wearing *Breakfast at Tiffany's* gloves—in August.

"Luanne! Are you still doing stand-up?" she said. I didn't bother to tell her she'd gotten my name wrong.

"I've taken some time off while I look for a day job," I said.

"Oh, tragic," she said. "I was hoping you'd be the one percent to make it." She patted my head like I was a toddler. "That's why I became a CPA. Well, that, and I'm not funny," she continued. Then she laughed at her own "joke" until she was red in the face. I poured myself another glass.

This crowd really made me appreciate my friends, a bunch of stand-up comics, artists, and advertising creatives who took risks and didn't choose their friends based on their tax brackets and golf scores. Even though some of them made six figures, they never slighted me for living at home.

The next thing I remember I was on the outdoor patio, where Emma was opening gifts in front of her fellow College of William and Mary graduates. She sat in a wicker chair that was custom made to look like a throne. Bright pink peonies and an ice sculpture of a stork carting a lifelike frozen baby in a blanket were just some of the added touches.

The glass table was piled high with gifts, so meticulously wrapped that I assumed they were done by a team of professionals, most likely flown in from a small third-world country. Emma held up a little wool sweater that was hand-knit by a girl named Claire. In fact, all the girls there seemed to be named Claire, except for the two who were named Margaret. They all had hyphenated last names and matching freckles. I'm short, brunette, and half-Irish, half-Sicilian. As I clutched my martini glass filled with whiskey, I felt like an oddball.

Emma held up a tiny windbreaker. The crowd cooed. "That's for her first sailing trip to Nantucket," said Margaret. This baby hadn't been born yet, and it already had the WASP agenda down. I had only been to the Jersey Shore. I finished the whiskey. Emma's long arms held up a card. "A helicopter ride," she said. Claire number two had purchased the fetus a trip in a chopper. Everyone clapped.

"That's stupid," I said. The crowd hushed. Each and every single pair of blue eyes was on me.

"Okay! Ha. Lianne is funny," Emma said.

"No, it's just fucking dumb," I slurred.

"No cussing," said the southernmost Claire. That's when I felt a gentle hand on the nape of my back. "Keep it going!" whispered the voice. It was Emma's fabulous gay cousin, Ben. She had told me a lot about him.

"Curse all you want," Ben's boyfriend said. "The three of us are out of place here."

I was so excited that "my people" had found me, and just when I needed them most. I was not going to let them down.

When Emma's mother-in-law rolled in a brand-new Bugaboo stroller, I took action. I stormed this high-end carriage like a drunken paratrooper. I took one look back at my two adoring fans, much like a prepubescent Olympic gymnast searching for her mother in the crowd just before mounting the balance beam. I dove butt-first into the stroller, but the wheels skidded across the floor and I landed on my coccyx bone. Everyone laughed, and I took that as a sign that I was winning the guests over. I leaped up and this time landed gracefully in the seat. With my petite frame, I fit comfortably and hung my feet over the front. "Ta-da, you guys!" I said.

"Lianne, please get out of the stroller," Emma said.

"I'll get up when everyone here can tell me what the inside of a soup kitchen looks like," I said. Meanwhile, I had never done volunteer work in my life.

The next thing I remember is lying down on a lounge chair in the private garden. Ben hovered over me. "Honey, that was brilliant what you did out there. You said what I was thinking. What a bunch of pretentious hens."

"Am I still here?" I slurred. My eyes were slits, and I was trying to make sense of my surroundings.

"Oh yeah, babe, they tried to kick you out but you couldn't walk. You've been out cold for two hours."

"I want to go home," I said.

"Why don't you sleep off the whiskey, and we'll help you out with that," he said.

I tried to pick my head up, but it bounced back down on the rubber lounge chair. "Close your legs, babe. Everyone can see your crotch," Ben advised, before heading back inside.

Next thing I knew I was lying on my back, staring at the night sky, when Emma appeared.

"How are you feeling?" she asked. That's when my stomach started to churn. It wasn't liking the white wine and whiskey. Like Bambi walking on ice, I got up and fell. Twice. I finally made it to the bathroom, where I projectile-vomited into the toilet. That's when my knight in pink gingham opened the door. I had flushed the toilet and was using the sink for balance.

"You okay?" Ben asked.

"Get me a roll!" I yelled. He dutifully returned with said bread product on a paper plate. I charged out of the bathroom ripping the roll with my teeth, much like a lion tears into a zebra carcass on *Animal Planet*. Naturally, there was a collective gasp from the remaining blue-bloods.

"Shut up, I'm going through a hard time," I said.

"She doesn't have a job," I heard Emma whisper.

"She lives with her parents, right?" asked one of the Claires. Then Emma's loving cousin and his boyfriend came to my final rescue. They swiftly carted me and the remaining half of my beloved carbohydrate out the door and to their apartment. That evening, I slept on a stark white Pottery Barn couch surrounded by two near strangers who accepted me at my worst.

The next morning I woke up and took in the giant poster of Donna Summer over the fireplace. Rainbow flags and watercolor paintings of the beaches of Provincetown were displayed on the mantel. I laughed out loud. The memories of the past evening came flooding back. I had made an epic fool of myself. But I knew I had gotten smashed because I felt inadequate.

Although my bad behavior was my fault, I'd allowed the crowd of lady Hitler Youths to exacerbate my disappointment in myself. I needed to use action, not liquor, to help improve my situation.

I vowed to make an effort not to lean on booze to escape anymore. I didn't respect those people, but I was no better than they were, acting like a drunken fool. I called Emma to apologize. As usual, she took the higher road and told me not to worry and that I added an "unexpected flavor" to her event.

Then I went to brunch with my new gay boyfriends. We drank Bloody Marys and cheered our newfound friendship.

"Emma's mother texted me to tell me that she thinks you need to go to AA," said Ben.

"Yeah, she needs to go to AA, allright—Assholes Anonymous. Those women suck," added his boyfriend.

"Not to the Claires!" I said as we clanked glasses.

Six years later, Emma is living in Greenwich, Connecticut, with her financier husband and three towheaded children. We hardly ever speak, but the gay boys and I carouse every now and again. Each time we hit up a Martini Monday drink special on the Lower East Side, I am reminded of how their friendship gave me strength during a tough time.

I still drink—sometimes like a sailor—but I imbibe to celebrate, not to avoid my misery. Booze is a fickle mistress, but if you let her, she'll teach you a valuable lesson.

THE SLIP

ANN LEARY

"MAY I OFFER YOU A tropical punch made with our own island rum?" asked the young hostess with the lovely West Indian accent. Then, smiling at our eleven-year-old son and nine-year-old daughter, she added, "Perhaps a fruit punch for the children?" My husband, Denis, grumbled a "no thanks" and stepped outside for a cigarette, but I said, "Yes, the kids and I would love a fruit punch. Thanks."

It had been a long trip. There was a layover in Miami and then a slow, hot drive across another island to a boat that took us to this island, and now we had to wait for our luggage to be transported to the resort. Somehow our bags had been sent to the wrong hotel. We had kids. We had stuff we needed. We were still dressed for winter, but it was eighty-five degrees outside and our room wasn't ready. My husband and I were barely speaking; the heat and exhaustion from racing through airports and tending to the children had made us revert to our favorite go-to coping device—blaming each other for everything that went wrong.

That morning, in Connecticut, we had begun the day, all four of us, eagerly anticipating a relaxing week in the sun. It was late February, and we had been wearing boots, coats, and mittens for months. Once I booked the flights, I had really not thought much about the logistics of getting to the resort. Somehow, I just had a vision of my family boarding an airplane and then running and laughing, all four of us, hand in hand, across a white sandy beach and then diving into the surf, where we would spend the entire week frolicking and splashing about like a family of playful seals. I had forgotten that we had a very tight window between the time we landed in Miami and the time we needed to board our flight to the island. Our flight out of JFK was delayed, and we missed the connecting flight. We had to wait in Miami for six hours until the next one. The children were restless. My husband felt the need to repeatedly interrogate me about my mind-set when I had booked the flights so close together. I silently interrogated myself about my mind-set when I had decided I would marry this tyrant.

But now, finally, we were in a tropical paradise with a cheerful, accommodating receptionist, and cool beverages were on their way. Within minutes a man appeared with three drinks on a tray. Two of them were bright pink and garnished with pineapple wedges. The third was a paler shade of pink and also had the pineapple garnish. The bright pink ones were handed to the kids. The third was for me. It appeared to be diluted with something. I pretended not to notice. I held my breath as I lifted the large glass to my lips so that I couldn't smell its contents. *Oops.* It tasted like there might be alcohol in it, but I wasn't sure, so I took another sip. Yes, it tasted like rum. I hadn't asked for the rum drink, so I took another sip to be absolutely certain. Yup, rum, allright. After all those years, I still recognized the lovely sweetness of rum and the warm way that it, like all spirits, made my heart feel, as if it might overflow with goodness.

Fourteen years earlier, at the age of twenty-four, I had slunk, absolutely sodden with shame and self-loathing, into a church basement to attend a meeting for alcoholics. Yes, one of *those* meetings, stocked with men and women who gathered regularly to "share their experience, strength, and hope with each other" to recover from alcoholism. It's an anonymous organization that prefers its members don't reveal their involvement in the fellowship on a public level; most of its members call it The Program. I had known about The Program ever since a friend's mother took me to my first meeting when I was eighteen. The mother was in The Program and believed, based on my drunken antics at her house and some stories that her daughter had shared with her, that I might benefit from The Program myself. I didn't. I was too young, but I was rather fascinated to learn that a few of my friends' parents were in this depressing program, where adults sat around in a circle and spoke in low tones and at times wept. My parents were out drinking that night, probably really tying one on, but Peggy Schumacher's mom was in the meeting, drinking coffee, and so was the guy who worked in our local grocery store.

Poor Peggy Schumacher's mom, I thought. *Poor guy from the market.* They were alcoholics, who would never be able to drink for the rest of their lives. You had to pity them.

For the next several years, I occasionally thought about the meeting and the people there. I felt very sorry for members of The Program, but though part of me always knew I drank differently than most others, I was certain that I wasn't an alcoholic. I went to college, held jobs. I had lots of friends. I just needed to control my drinking. My friends all liked to drink, but somehow on most occasions I was the one nobody was speaking to the next day. I was a blackout drinker from the very first time I drank in junior high school, so I often didn't have any recollection of what I had done to enrage my friends. We had all been having drinks. I was feeling great. I loved my friends, loved myself. I would often express my love for my fellows and myself, and then it was the next morning and my friends were not speaking to me and I hated myself again.

My friend Lauren tried to help me sort it all out one day. "The problem with you is that you just don't know when to stop. After two or three drinks, I start to get that out-of-control feeling, and I realize it's time to switch to water. I think that's what you need to do."

I remember nodding tearfully. I was reeling with shame about some incident from the night before, but in all honesty, I had no idea what she was talking about. After two or three drinks, I always start to feel *in* control, but how do you explain to a social drinker what it's like to have been born three drinks short of comfortable? You can't.

When I stopped drinking at age twenty-four, I went to another meeting. This time I heard what all the other people born three drinks short were saying, and I realized that I had found my tribe. I had always loved boozers when I was drinking. I'd single them out at parties within seconds and plant myself next to them—the *fun* people—and now here were the same characters, sans booze but *avec* the warped perspectives, maladaptive coping skills, and hysterical stories about how they came to be in The Program. I found myself shoulder to shoulder with my brethren—all the disappointed dreamers—the type of people who imagine themselves running along beaches holding hands with their loved ones and then are blindsided by the logistics of getting from one place to another. I learned in The Program that I drank to cope with the disappointments of life and that I needed meetings to help me to live "life on life's terms" (another corny cult slogan), not based on my own childish fantasies about how life should be.

When I stopped drinking, there was some joy and relief each morning when I woke up and remembered going to bed the night before, but I missed it. A lot. The topography of the dry world, especially during those early months, was so strange and foreign that it was sometimes hard to find my bearings. So, like an expat who has found herself in a sometimes beautiful but often frightening new world, I liked to meet up with people from my soggy homeland and remind myself why I had left. Nothing worked where I came from; everything was broken. I talked about this fact with writers, artists, bankers, ex-cons, current felons, grannies, junkies, and the occasional movie star who frequented meetings of The Program that I attended every day. Truly, the most interesting people I have known, I met in those meeting halls. My new friends and I all made fun of the corniness of the slogans and the literature, but at the same time we clung to the ridiculously simplistic tenets of the program ("One day at a time"; "Easy does it") and lived by them.

"You gotta be neck-deep in this thing if you wanna get better," an aging bookie told me at one of my first meetings. Soon I was, and my life did get better. My relationship with Denis—at that time my live-in boyfriend—improved. We got married, we had two great kids, Denis's career took off, and we were no longer broke. We moved to Manhattan and later Connecticut. I had been sober about eight years (one day at a time!) when I stopped going to meetings.

I stopped going for many reasons. First, it was hard to find the time. When I had an hour or two away from the kids, I wanted to do other things that seemed more important. Also, I started to worry about other parents seeing me coming in and out of church basements with big A triangles hanging from the doors. Before I had kids, while we were living in Boston, I didn't mind if people knew that I was in The Program. I didn't need to explain to anybody why I was there, because my friends all knew what I was like when I drank. But in New York and Connecticut, nobody had ever seen me drunk. When my new friends asked why I didn't drink, I said that I had been a little wild when I was younger and that I just liked my life better without drinking. Most people were fine with that explanation, but several friends told me that they, too, had been wild in their youth, also binge drinkers who occasionally suffered blackouts, but that they had grown out of that behavior. "When I became a mom, I changed," a friend told me. "I could never party now the way I used to. I just have a glass of wine or two with my husband at dinner. Maybe a couple drinks at a party. That's it."

I didn't drink for another five years, but during those years I started entertaining the fantasy that I might be able to become a social drinker, had I given myself time to mature. The thing that kept me from helping myself to my husband's vodka or ordering a drink when I was out with friends was The Program. I had been programmed not to drink. In The Program they say that "the first drink gets you drunk," and I had become terrified of taking that first drink. In my mind, after that first drink, all bets were off. If I had even one glass of wine, I would be compelled to have another and another until I awoke from a blackout behind prison bars. My children would be in the custody of Child Protective Services, where they would remain until my husband could be located. I am not exaggerating; that is how fearful of alcohol I had become. To choose to take a drink was to choose to destroy my life and my family.

That hot day at the island resort, however, I hadn't chosen to take a drink. I had asked for a fruit punch, and they had misunderstood. On another day, in another place, if I had been rested and well fed, if I weren't enraged at my husband and fed up with my children, I would have asked the waiter what was in the drink as soon as I saw its color. That day I didn't. I hadn't asked for a drink, but here I was sipping one.

It was an accident.

After my second or third sip, I decided to turn it into an experiment. An alcoholic would be compelled to order another drink, and then another and another, after that first rum punch. I left the drink half-full on the reception desk when the valet led us to our rooms, and I didn't look back. When he showed us the complimentary bottle of island rum that sat on top of the refrigerator, I barely glanced at it. I didn't feel like having that rum. An alcoholic would have opened the bottle and started chugging its contents the moment her husband turned his back. I suggested we all go to the beach for a swim, and for the rest of that day I swam and strolled on the beach in a sort of daze, filled with a sense of euphoric wonder. It seemed that I could have one drink after all. I *could* stop drinking once I started. Perhaps I was not an alcoholic. Later that night, I tested my hypothesis by pouring a slug of the free rum into my Coke and sipping it before we headed down to dinner. I didn't want another drink at dinner. It was official. I was not an alcoholic. It felt then that I had been living some sort of stagnant half-life for years, but now I was whole again. I had been enslaved by the tyranny of the cultish Program, but now I was free.

I didn't tell my husband about my discovery until we returned to Connecticut. It had been fourteen years since he had seen me drunk. At first he was skeptical, but after spending a few nights with the new me, I had him convinced that I could drink again. For some people, alcohol lessens their inhibitions and makes their sex life more interesting. I'm rather uninhibited naturally—my baseline is just a hair above an exhibitionist—and when I drink I'm what a former boyfriend once called "a bit of a handful but lots of fun," so who could blame my husband for overlooking, with me, the obvious signs that I was not really in control of my drinking at all? We started having all that fun with my being a handful again. Plus, he was away a lot of the time, so he didn't see me drunk on a regular basis, and I was careful that the kids and my friends didn't either. I would pour a glass of wine while cooking dinner for the kids and then refill it only when they were out of the room. That way it looked like I was drinking the same glass of wine all night, when in truth I often consumed quite a lot more. When I was out with friends I never had more than two glasses of wine. I had to drive home and wasn't going to drive while intoxicated. That's what alcoholics did. After I arrived home, checked on my sleeping children, and sent the babysitter on her way, I would enjoy a bottle on my own.

Here's the strangest thing: Though I had attended meetings for years and had read dozens of books on the subjects of alcoholism, addiction, and recovery, once I started drinking again, I was unable to recognize the signs of my own alcoholism. I truly believed I was in control of my drinking. When I had my moments of doubt, I made excuses. I hadn't eaten enough. Everybody was drunk at that party. I'm a grown-up! Grown-ups sometimes get drunk! To view my drinking as normal, I had to view the perspective of The Program as completely warped. I had been like a dependent child when I had been in The Program. I had been brainwashed into thinking that I had a drinking problem, when really, I assured myself, I drank like most other adults. In The Program, people talked about how once you had a slip, you would lose everything you had gained in your sobriety. It would be a fast downhill slide straight to the gutter. I had my first book published during those few years I returned to drinking. I went on a book tour and attended book parties, very careful to stick to the two- or three-glass maximum while out. My life got *better* when I drank, which was proof enough that I wasn't an alcoholic.

Right? I asked myself as I poured the last drops of a bottle into my glass, all alone in the dark with my dogs. *Right?* I asked as I staggered to the fridge for a fresh bottle. *Right?* I asked as my daughter inadvertently crashed my party of one and found me stumbling toward her, trying to talk but unable to arrange my mouth so that it could form the words properly.

I've been back in the cultish, corny, lifesaving Program for six years.

One damned blessed day at a time.

"MY NAME IS AMY F."

AMY FERRIS

HI, MY NAME IS AMY F.

And I am an . . .

Okay, I'm not an alcoholic.

I'm not.

No, I'm not.

I'm what you call a daily drinker. At five o'clock every day, I pour myself a glass of wine. White wine, preferably a pinot grigio or sauvignon blanc. I don't like chardonnay or riesling. However, truth be told, after, say, eight o'clock, either tastes fine.

I'm not picky after eight.

I started drinking when I gave up smoking. I also stopped having sex on a regular basis and, truth be told, I began Googling old boyfriends in the middle of the night. But this isn't about that. This is about drinking.

Well, actually . . . that's not completely true. It's about not feeling good enough. Not feeling enough. Not feeling important enough or special enough. Smoking kept me at arm's length, kept me from being intimate even in a crowd or a group of people. When you don't feel you're enough, you keep people at a distance.

I actually found solace and comfort in drinking. It seemed like something I could do alone. Without much explanation or fanfare. Without permission.

My dad died eleven years ago. When he died, I was an occasional drinker. I drank maybe a glass of wine every few days. After his death, my family began to unravel.

Slowly.

My father held us together like glue.

More like Elmer's Glue, not Krazy Glue.

But I didn't know that then.

I know it now.

He loved family. He loved having family get-togethers, having his family sitting around a Passover table or a Thanksgiving table. This brought him joy.

I would categorize my mother and father as occasional drinkers. Their wine color of choice was red. I believe, although I could be wrong, that my father preferred Demerol, Percodan, or Percocet to alcohol. My mother preferred smoking and screaming and slamming doors.

My father died.

I began drinking.

Slowly.

I liked the feeling of disappearing into my own thoughts. My own pain. My own memories of him. I liked suppressing my sadness. And the reason I liked suppressing my feelings was because neither my mother nor my brother wanted to talk about my dad. The conversation went like this:

"Mom, I miss Daddy."

"Amy, I don't want to talk about this. It's much too sad for me."

"I'm sad, too, Mom."

"I know. But I don't want to talk about this. I just can't."

"Okay."

"Okay."

Everyone seemed to want to make his life—my dad's life—disappear. Poof. Gone. Bye.

Okay. I can do that, too. I can push the cork back in the bottle, push it down hard and tight, and get on with my life.

I could disappear, too, into my life.

I wrote a young-adult book. I wrote a few movies. Ken, my husband, and I were happy. And yes, God yes, I had a good life.

And then I began another journey. Menopause. Oh my fucking God. Menopause. Just when you think everything is fine, good, safe, okay—it grabs you by the throat and squeezes the life out of you.

I began drinking more. And let me just say for the record, with menopause comes memory loss, so I don't really remember how much I was drinking, but I'm betting it was between two and four glasses a night. White wine. On top of my dad dying, my family unraveling bit by bit, I encountered menopause just as my mother encountered dementia.

A fucking collision course.

I did not want to feel anything. My therapist asked me what I was trying to achieve, and I told her I wanted to understand what it was like to be in a coma but still be able to apply makeup and get dressed.

She told me I was feeling invisible, as if no one was paying attention to me. This is very common among women my age, she explained.

FYI: Midlife is not unlike puberty. Not at all. It's exactly the same but with cellulite. I was feeling and experiencing what I had felt as a teenager. Honest to God, it was almost identical. I felt unattractive, unwanted, self-conscious. I felt like an outcast. Like the gawky girl who wore upper and lower braces. Wine—sipping, drinking wine. Holding that glass by the stem kept me from exposing the painful truth—my lack of confidence and my self-loathing.

I learned that even standing in a corner, wedged between the wall and the bookshelves, you can be very sloppy, tripping over your own heels, not to mention your own words. Feeling invisible but not acting invisible.

The thing is—what I've learned—people don't often stop you from drinking in public places. It's not that they're unkind or mean-spirited. It's just easier to not say anything to your face. It's safer to keep a distance. Folks often talk about you (you know, you in general) behind your back. I know I've done it. When a friend of mine became a serious drinker, we—her friends—all commiserated on the phone or at a restaurant, saying how awful it was, how sloppy and weird she'd become, how messy and unattractive. But no one, not one person, called her to say, "You need help."

I decided I didn't want to be that type of person anymore. I didn't want to be the one talking behind anyone's back, particularly when someone I loved was clearly unable to control herself. I let my friend know that she was walking on a cliff, and I didn't want her to fall off.

Let me now introduce you to Richard. He and his wife, Rebecca, are two unique, funny, charming, down-to-earth people. Theirs is a sexy, loving marriage. Filled with quirks and winks and great humor.

Richard, a former chief economist with the Securities and Exchange Commission and a professor at the Yale School of Management, is the kind of guy who doesn't bullshit or beat around the bush. He also happens to be one of the more intelligent human beings on this planet. He's often quoted in magazines and newspapers, and he speaks in front of thousands of people who want his advice and wisdom and who hang on his every word.

We were, the four of us—Ken and I, Richard and Rebecca—having a "first date" of sorts.

Now, let me just say that with my dad's death came the desire and ability to push down my fears. My worries. Drinking helped me do that. If I felt sad, unhappy, angry, disappointed, confused, doubtful, a drink would distance me from those feelings.

And another piece of the equation that came to the surface full force was my own lack of confidence, my insecurities. I often felt less than. I dropped out of high school, and for years I felt deep shame about that. Coupled with that shame came a real sense of inferiority. Dropping out of high school has the same sort of ring as "Hey, I spent a few years in prison."

I don't like small intimate events with folks I hardly know. I feel like I have to watch myself and be aware of every single thing I do and say. I prefer to lose myself in a crowd. I head right for a corner. Tuck myself in, and I don't worry about falling. I have a wall to hold me up.

Okay, so the dinner will be just the four of us. Immediately I begin to panic. What to wear? What to talk about?

I tell Ken to call the dinner off.

Right now.

He says no. He likes Rebecca. He and Rebecca have much to talk about. They both love gardening. He and Rebecca can talk about composting and soil and bulbs and trees and planting and weeding for three, four, five hours. It's called a common thread. I don't garden, so that's a conversation I won't be able to contribute to. However, I can talk about buying flowers.

I want to feel better. I want my heart to stop racing. I can feel every insecurity bubble up to the surface. I tell myself to push it down. I tell myself to wear something fabulous so I can hide my feelings.

I get dressed. I look good. I wear flats so I won't wobble (no doubt I will have more than two glasses of wine) if I have to go to the ladies' room.

We arrive at the restaurant, one of our local favorites, and soon realize that not only is this going to be an intimate dinner but no one else is at the restaurant. The weather is horrible. Heavy rains.

Richard and Rebecca arrive. We sit at a corner table and open the two bottles of wine that they bring: one red, one white. Richard tells us that the white is a very good wine—a crisp and smooth white—and the red is one of his favorites. We toast. Ken and Rebecca immediately get going on the gardening chatter. I turn to Richard and want to kick-start a conversation. I want desperately to say something smart, funny, intelligent. Honest to God, I bring up the weather. I say something like, "Can you believe this rain?" I stop sipping the wine and start pouring it down my throat.

And this is what I say to myself: *Amy, say something funny. Funny always works.*

I say something funny. Smart and funny. Richard laughs. Ken and Rebecca both laugh, and we start talking. And then, as in most conversations, there's an awkward lull. Uncomfortable, I slink down a bit in the chair. I pour myself a little more wine. And then I watch and listen to the three of them talking. The more I distance myself, the harder it is to jump back in, and the harder it is to jump back in, the more I want to hide.

Disappear.

I can feel myself getting emotionally wobbly. I'm not quite drunk. I'm on the cusp. The owner of the restaurant comes over, and a conversation begins. Not a topic I feel confident enough to jump in on.

There's no more wine. The bottles are empty.

I ask the owner for "another glass of white, please."

I feel like Oliver Twist in the movie: "More, sir. Can I have some more?"

In that moment, without anyone else noticing except me, Richard shakes his head ever so slightly.

So kind.

So loving.

So subtle.

There was nothing embarrassing about it. Nothing humiliating. It was personal, private.

In that moment he saved me from making a fool of myself. It's not that I would have said something foolish. No, no. God, no. It's that I would have been sloppy. And I would have hated myself in the morning. And I would have berated myself and continued feeling inferior.

It's always the next morning that's filled with rewinding and replays and "if onlys."

In that moment I knew, deeply, that someone—Richard—was paying great attention to me.

I was no longer invisible.
I still drink wine.
But I no longer feel I have nothing to say.
I have a lot to say.
Hello, my name is Amy Ferris.

THE ROOT CELLAR

RITA WILLIAMS

BECAUSE OF THE DEEP freezes of Colorado winters, we had to keep the wine crocks down in the root cellar underground. The dandelion wine was my favorite. Not too sweet—a clear pale gold. We plucked the slender petals from the flower heads at high noon in midsummer to trap the sun's warmth for the dark winter that lurked above our little house for nine long months. It never failed. When the wine hit, I shuddered—then the heat wound its way up my spine and out the tips of my fingers and the very ends of my hair.

The brilliant pollen in the wine made me a little crazy—enough to laugh out loud at the blizzard shrieking above, me in the stillness of a tomb. The fancy ski tourists had no idea that every single Colorado winter, somebody froze. The previous month they'd found Snowball, the town drunk, frozen solid on the Trailways bus bench, a bottle of Silver Satin wine clutched in his fist. But after my chores, I couldn't resist secreting myself away for a half hour and pouring the elixir of yellow blossoms down my throat, until I finally wasn't cold, and then taking out his picture. Another sip and I could find that place inside myself, when it was summer and I saw the ballet and that dancer.

The dance camp only lasted six short weeks. My aunt and I cleaned the toilets there—mopped the theaters, the dance studios, the dressing rooms smelling of paint. The dancers arrived in June from New York, Chicago, and Los Angeles, with their new leotards and bottles of shampoo and letters from worried mothers and shoe-boxes full of toiletries and cookies and warm socks and dental floss. I had never heard of dental floss.

They came to study art. I thought that meant paintings, but it turned out dance was art, too. Painting with the body, I guessed. They stalked about, their gazes fixed as if dance were a religion—ballet and modern, primary sects. So urgent about it. Emphatic that "modern" was a very real thing.

The dance studio had taken root in the middle of a field, waist-high, sea-green hay, dancers swaying to the études winding their way out of the tinny little piano. And the soft-skinned aspen trees with their blackened scars stood stock still, watching. The roof, corrugated tin, kept the dancers dry in the rains, cool on the hot days.

I have the photo they took of him that day, doing that arabesque. Although the picture is black and white and one corner is curled and charred, I remember him leaping through the cobalt sky above the grass—the black tights, his torso, his arched foot like a blade. The smell of the fire remains buried in the photo.

Toleda was one of the cooks at the camp. She was tall, sapling thin, the color of pine bark, with small, wary, intelligent eyes that didn't care for me from the start. With her bristling thistle stance. Her thin songs about Jesus saving her when I could see the sadness trapped in her long brown neck. Her wig with the bun that didn't set right. Stubbles at her hairline like coiled principles still waiting to be unwound. Her pruny thumbs fingering the ruffled lettuces that we brought to camp from our garden, especially for the "salad girl," because homegrown stuff was particularly tender. Peeling radishes into little roses and making certain all her tomato slices were uniform. Proud that she could still work in her eighties. Immensely proud of her signature, snowy starched aprons. The old kind of starch from paste, not the spray can. Every morning she'd come in smelling freshly ironed, ruffles around the bottom and the sleeves. And the strings—somehow she managed to tie them behind her in a big snowy bow.

She was down at the main house alone that morning, supposedly making Miss Helen biscuits. Miss Helen, the camp administrator, was just back from a trip around the world and ready for some home cooking, but for some reason she had gone on up to the lodge.

Nobody else but me knows exactly how it happened. I was supposed to first go to the main house to drop off some dandelion wine for Toleda that morning, along with a flat of fresh raspberries. But then I thought, *Who'll notice if I'm a little late?* So I sneaked off to the dance studio in the middle of the field. With a big thunderstorm coming that day, how could I miss that dancer?

Toleda would have been singing these "Precious blood never failed me yet" songs. Having been raised Catholic, I didn't get it. We'd kneel and mumble, "Mea culpa, mea culpa, mea maxima culpa." Through my fault, through my fault, through my most grievous fault. And, "Oh, my God, I am heartily sorry for having offended thee!" The dripping blood from the altar that we were supposed to drink, and the flesh of his body. Well, it was a very different tone than the states she'd chant herself into, shouting in that tuneless ropy voice, "Yes, Jesus, yes!"

Once, Toleda caught me studying her and flinched. "Hussy. You may think you white. But you gon' find out you a Negro just like me." I felt scalded. Because I had been wondering exactly how black I was. And whether I was lost, too. But we were different. I was certain neither Jesus nor anybody else was going to save me. But I was also certain I was born to be a dancer, that those dancers, even if they were white, were my tribe. More so than she, even though we were both black.

With a huff, Toleda swirled around with those great snowy ruffles—much the same as she must have done that morning—turning her back to that hulking, hissing stove with its eight burners, its blue pilot flame recessed just out of sight under the heavy grates. Sweat blistered her smooth forehead, spilling into her eyes, obscuring her vision. Circling from the counter where she'd been rolling out the biscuits, down to the oven, and back to the dough. Then on to the bacon and carefully tucking the biscuits into the tray so the edges didn't touch. Singing away: "One thing I know, he loves me so." Then pausing to ponder where she might have stashed the raspberry jam that Miss Helen favored—the jam she had to keep hiding from the dancers who slipped in to steal it. Raspberry jam we'd made and brought, that I was supposed to have given her that morning, along with that last bottle of dandelion wine.

That burning smell most likely didn't seem like much. Probably the long starched apron strings caught fire first. And since the room was already hot, she may have missed the intent of the blaze nibbling its way up until it attached itself to that wig. That wig with the chignon like a doorknob at the nape of her neck, where the flame could ease its way in.

She had the presence of mind to run into the den, grab one of the Navajo blankets down from the wall, and roll in it. Who knows how long it took before she was able to crawl out to the road where they found her. Or how it might have gone had I been where I was supposed to be.

Much later, when I'd gone down there to clean, I found the cindered biscuits, burned like bitter stones. Remnants of scorched cloth and skin littered the flour board, where she'd just created a well in the flour. An overturned can of baking powder spilled. Clabbering milk slick on the floor. Somehow I didn't really believe she was gone until I saw that. She'd always been so immaculate, with her implements hanging according to size, wiping down all her spice cans daily, arranging all her vinegars with the labels facing out, weaving her little life adjacent to those of the soaring dancers.

I noticed his photo at the edge of the table, where Miss Helen was supposed to see it that morning. I scraped off the cinders, and, shame roaring in my ears, I tucked it inside my shirt.

In the root cellar, I kept the photo behind the crocks of wine, pressed between the leaves of that summer's dance program, *The*

Rise of the Minoans. In the light of the coal oil lantern, the picture of him doing that arabesque eventually cracked in the brittle cold. I had to be very, very careful not to break it with my thick and clumsy mittens. Still, I had my own faith. Holding on to those crocks that made up my bar—the sanded beets, carrots, parsnips, potatoes on the right, wines on the left—I did the pliés and relevés I'd seen him doing, with my spine as straight as Toleda's might have been. I wished the picture no longer smelled of the fire. But even the living sun in the cup of dandelion wine could not take it all away.

DRINKING AS GENUINE VOCATION

JANE FRIEDMAN

THE FIRST BOOK I READ that changed my worldview was *Demian,* by Hermann Hesse. It opens like this: "I wanted only to try to live in accord with the promptings which came from my true self. Why was that so very difficult?"

This was fifteen years before I discovered that drinking is one path to uncovering the true self. But such a realization never would have come without this book's priming me for the insight. Hesse's novel focuses on how we must each confront and accept our shadow self, that part of our being that we do everything to repress and even project onto others.

Many people are afraid of their shadows in the same way they're afraid of drinking. There's a risk. What if we cede control? What if we don't like ourselves? What if we in fact lose ourselves? I have found myself to be the rare advocate of opening up a big bottle of alcohol to see how fast I can lose my precious "self." Drinking lets me play at seeing just how far out I can get from my "self"—or just how close.

The fear of losing ourselves is a curious one. How could we ever be anything but ourselves, in every thought and action? If one really meditates on that notion, it can be terrifying. What I mean is: Are you able to accept, at the deepest level, that every single thing you've done is really *you?* It's not something apart from you. It's not the "you" that's separate because it's undesirable or undergoing self-improvement. It's all every bit *you.*

If I start to think that it was really *me* who stole quarters from my mother's purse, or *me* who cheated on my husband, or *me* who broke off a friendship cold, my first instinct is to find a way to defend the action. But to accept my shadow, I've had to stop defending and start opening. Drinking helps me open more.

However, some people drink as a method of defense and refuse to open. If not prepared to gaze upon the layers of sweetness and stench, you can use drinking as a method of total self-annihilation. This isn't such a bad thing. We secretly love to smash things we create, including ourselves, and destruction plays an essential role in the happiest of lives. "Whoever wants to be born, must destroy a world," Hesse said. I admit to having used alcohol with this intention—to give myself permission to delve into the darkness and come out with the dawn holding a fresh view.

My first dark dive was during my junior year in college, when I welcomed a visit from a radio engineer who'd been sweet on me for years. He brought a bottle of wine, probably knowing that I needed encouragement. I drank too much and too fast, but instead of feeling more relaxed and carefree, I started to think about my first love from high school. We had broken up six months prior, but I was convinced he was the only one I should be with. How could I betray my one and only first love?

The wine helped. Before long I was heaving over the sink as the radio engineer (my second lover of all time) held my hair out of the way. The dark reality I faced that night was that I'd always compare the one I was with to the love who came before.

The concept of the shadow essentially taught me that you can't have light without darkness—one implies the other—just as with the yin and the yang. Contrary forces are intertwined. And drinking is the perfect vehicle for revealing this truth about life. Charles Coulombe says in his book *The Muse in the Bottle*, "In one night—even in one drink—one's emotions can run the whole gamut, from love to hate to fear. One's dignity dissolves, or is rediscovered; one escapes responsibility, or embraces it . . . almost all of the darkest [moments] carry some hint of redemption." This perfectly describes one of the most memorable nights of my life.

After more than a decade of working in publishing, I was leaving for the academic world. On the last day of my employment, for four hours in the evening, I drank with the people who would soon be my former colleagues. I never loved and enjoyed them more than I did then; we made all kinds of promises to remain close. When I got home, I cried for all that was lost, and also for fear of what lay ahead. The next morning, life continued with all those emotions integrated—appreciation and love for what had come before, and acceptance of fear as an inevitable part of change.

I'm wary of people who swear off drinking. It's like swearing off the experience of life and holding on too tight to the illusion of control. There are exceptions, of course, the most obvious being people who've had trouble with drinking in the past. Just as Mr. Kurtz, in Conrad's *Heart of Darkness,* wholly succumbed to the darkness, some wholly succumb to the bottle. Those who find the light again after prolonged darkness can feel an urgency to warn others about the danger.

I once had a stranger email me about my publicly proclaimed drinking habit. He wrote:

> *Listen, I don't want you to drink. I've been where you're at. It's a "brief vacation," and something you feel entitled to, and a chance to be yourself. What it's doing is taking away time you could be falling in love. Finding an important relationship is a job—it takes time and effort. And drinking is a job. How many jobs can you hold? How much time have you got in your life?*
>
> *Anywhere alcohol takes you is bullshit. You say things you don't mean, make promises you forget to keep, make resolutions that are worthless, and think of things to write*

that are crap. When I drank, I was really hurting from a sense
of loss (and it wasn't because my marriage failed). Now, I'm
in love with my wife and I don't want to ruin it by drinking.

Drinking can bring all kinds of behavior to the surface, and bullshit or not, those behaviors are still an expression of yourself, a chance to uncover or reveal something that might otherwise remain hidden. If you don't like what issues forth—if you don't think it represents your "true" self—then it's like denying you've got a rascal inside, just like everyone else. Drinking brushes away that pretty curtain we've made, and when the curtain parts too wide, our first inclination is to secure it better the next time. But I'm a writer, and writers are born to look behind the curtain.

Drinking has the added bonus of easing the human preoccupation with self-awareness. This awareness is a problem and a burden, and what F. Scott Fitzgerald must have been suffering from when he said, "My stories written when sober are stupid. . . . All reasoned out, not felt." Just as writers can produce mechanical work by overthinking, so, too, can we lead mechanical lives by overthinking our actions.

I frequently run into this problem at work functions, where I'm surrounded by acquaintances. One time, not long after I'd received a promotion at work, I was forced to sit at the CEO's table during a formal dinner. Had I been sober, I would've been so critically self-aware that I wouldn't have spoken a word. But with a few drinks in me, I became a better listener and empathizer. When the CEO made an offhand comment, I caught a sudden glimpse of the man behind the label, and for a moment I felt a kinship. I made a small comment to him, a subtle wink at what I'd glimpsed—and his eyes lit up. Because drinking helped unchain me from thoughts of *poor little me* and inspired grander idealism, I allowed the possibility of something in common with a CEO. And there was—of course there was!

I've always secretly thrilled at the thought that Alan Watts, an enlightened person and great spiritual teacher admired by many, likely drank himself to death. I like to think he drank because alcohol helped him, as it helps me, focus on the ecstasy of what's just right here, without the echo chamber of the mind going on and on and on. When I drink, I feel more myself, without hang-ups, without getting stuck. I observe it all the more deeply and feel it all the more acutely—and in this, perhaps, I am like every other desperate writer, looking for the next remarkable thought.

William James said, "One of the charms of drunkenness unquestionably lies in the deepening sense of reality and truth which is gained therein. In whatever light things may then appear to us, they seem more utterly what they are, more 'utterly utter' than when we are sober."

But critics of drinking love to focus on the wild card in all this, something that Coulombe points out: Drinking can gild ordinary experience with deeper reality *as well as* illusion. We can end up in a maudlin state, where affection and love for every human being in proximity or even in memory bubble to the surface. But is it an authentic emotion or an illusion manufactured by alcohol?

Just as we're afraid of bringing forth the darkness when we drink, we're also suspicious of positive emotion flowing without reservation. We suspect anything that hasn't been rationally produced and analyzed, so we run our emotional reactions through the scientific method.

No wonder people drink to escape.

There's a famous quote from Nietzsche about drinking. He says, "For art to exist, for any sort of aesthetic activity to exist, a certain physiological precondition is indispensable: intoxication." Unfortunately, this quote rarely includes the sentence immediately following: "In this condition, one enriches everything out of one's own abundance; what one sees, what one desires, one sees swollen, pressing, strong, overladen with energy."

If that's an illusion, I'm going to encourage it along. I wouldn't drink if it weren't encouraging an abundance of thought and emotion that I wouldn't ordinarily experience. And while this essay was written outside the influence of alcohol, the person who exists to write it in this moment is someone who exists in a state of abundance, in part due to the experiences granted from intoxication.

Of course, it's just as easy to end up in a diminished and melancholy state, where every idea that crosses the mind becomes a depressing touch point—every event a loss, every relationship a fraud, every achievement a disappointment. Whoever coined the phrase about drinking to drown your sorrows must not have been a very experienced drunk. For me, drinking is more likely to amplify sorrows and prompt newly imagined ones. Which reminds me of how, one weekday night, nearly a year and a half after my divorce, I consumed a 750-millileter bottle of Chimay and performed my first and last drunken dial, to my ex-husband. I felt as if he were the only one who could console me after a terrible incident with my mother and that if I did call him, he'd invite me right over.

He did not invite me right over.

At any moment in time, sober or drunk, we can play Jekyll or we can play Hyde. We can shine a light or we can explore the darkness. The dualism elicited by alcohol reveals our core nature because we drop our defenses against it—our rational, order-seeking, critical voice finally shuts up. When we drink to the bottom of the barrel and unguardedly explore the edges of the universe of ourselves, and find the extreme edge where we don't recognize what we are anymore, we realize there is no true self at all that we can pin down. It is, at heart, an illusion.

When we drink, we get a glimpse of how ridiculous we can be in our efforts to try to "keep it together." We don't really keep ourselves together—we shift, we change, we stop, start, end, and begin again. This is why I've never taken drinking seriously. I do not treat it as something about which I must be careful or presume that I can pluck only the sublime parts of it while leaving behind the undesirable side effects. It is all the experience of life, and if I'm paying attention, then every moment can be accepted as part of what I am and what this existence is.

I've often wondered, though: Once you receive the message, is it time to hang up the phone?

The process of encountering and integrating our shadow selves isn't a one-time event but a journey and lifelong process. But even if it isn't, I can't give up drinking, not yet. I can't let go of how, in my best drunken moments, everything that's beautiful about a person comes into sharper focus. As writer Art Hill says, "This capacity to invest the ordinary or the ugly with an aura of beauty . . . is the one positive justification ever put forward for the alcoholic's addiction."

Drinking always reminds me of how deeply I've loved—and how I love still, even if I'm the only one to know it. Even if I've sworn off all fond feelings for a person, a little bit of bourbon fills me with affection again. I don't hesitate to keep drinking, wandering through darkness and light. Because, as Hesse says, each person has only one genuine vocation: to find the way to himself.

CONTRIBUTORS

SARI BOTTON's articles and essays have appeared in *The New York Times*, *Harper's Bazaar*, *More*, *W*, *New York*, *Good Housekeeping*, *Marie Claire*, the *New York Daily News*, *Time Out New York*, *The Village Voice*, The Rumpus.net, This Recording.com, and various anthologies. She's taught at SUNY–Albany and is a partner in the TMI Project, a nonprofit that empowers teens and adults in need through writing workshops. Sari is also a *New York Times* bestselling ghostwriter.

SAMANTHA DUNN is the author of several books, including the novel *Failing Paris*, a finalist for the PEN Center fiction award, and the memoir *Not by Accident: Reconstructing a Careless Life*. Her essays have been widely anthologized; she coedited the collection *Women on the Edge: Writing from Los Angeles*. She teaches in the UCLA Writers' Program and is the adviser for PEN Center's The Mark, a program to help new writers complete finished books. She lives in Southern California with her husband and their son, Benen.

ADRIENNE EDENBURN-MACQUEEN has spent a fair portion of her twenty-six years treating her body with the same care and compassion usually reserved for a rest stop on the New Jersey Turnpike, making it out with relatively few scars. One night, after a fight with a now-forgotten boyfriend, she sat down and wrote an essay about her sobriety, which won *Glamour* magazine's annual essay contest. She lives in Connecticut, where she works as a waitress and is writing her first book, a memoir.

AMY FERRIS is an author, screenwriter, playwright, and editor. Her memoir, *Marrying George Clooney: Confessions from a Midlife Crisis* (Seal Press), opened off-Broadway in March 2012. She is co-editor of a new anthology, *Dancing at the Shame Prom* (Seal Press). Amy is a champion of all things women-centric. She lives in Pennsylvania with her husband, Ken. She's quite happy with how her life turned out.

JANE FRIEDMAN serves as the web editor for the *Virginia Quarterly Review* and blogs on writing and new media at JaneFriedman .com. Her expertise on technology and publishing has been featured by *NPR, PBS,* and *Publishers Weekly,* and she has spoken at more than two hundred events about writing and the digital age. Before joining *VQR,* Jane was the publisher of *Writer's Digest* and also served as an assistant professor of e-media at the University of Cincinnati.

BECKY SHERRICK HARKS is a bachelor's-prepared nurse and freelance writer living in Chicago with her three small, yet very loud, children. When she's not running her nonprofit organization, the Band Back Together Project, or writing on her award-winning blog, MommyWantsVodka.com, she enjoys pretending to be married to men from television, dreaming about aerosolized frosting, and competitive napping.

KATHRYN HARRISON is the author of the novels *Enchantments, Envy, The Seal Wife, The Binding Chair, Poison, Exposure,* and *Thicker Than Water.* She has also written memoirs: *The Kiss, The Mother Knot,* and *The Road to Santiago,* a travel memoir, as well as a biography, *Saint Thérèse of Lisieux,* a collection of personal essays, *Seeking Rapture,* and a work of true crime, *While They Slept: An Inquiry into the Murder of a Family.* Harrison is a frequent reviewer for *The New York Times Book Review.* Her essays have appeared in many publications, including *The New Yorker, Vogue,* and *Harper's.* She lives in

New York with her husband, the novelist Colin Harrison, and their children. She is currently at work on a biography of Joan of Arc.

SUSAN HENDERSON is a two-time Pushcart Prize nominee and the recipient of an Academy of American Poets award. Her debut novel, *Up from the Blue* (HarperCollins), was selected as a Great Group Reads pick (by the Women's National Book Association), an outstanding softcover release (by NPR), a Best Bets Pick (by *BookReporter*), an Editor's Pick (by BookMovement), an Editor's Choice (by BookBrowse), a Prime Reads pick (by HarperCollins New Zealand), a Top 10 of 2010 (by Shelf Awareness), and a favorite-reads feature on *The Rosie O'Donnell Show*. Susan blogs at www.litpark.com.

ANN HOOD is the author, most recently, of the novels *The Knitting Circle* and *The Red Thread* and a memoir, *Comfort: A Journey Through Grief*, which was a *New York Times* Editors' Choice and was chosen as one of the top ten nonfiction books of 2008 by *Entertainment Weekly*.

PAM HOUSTON is the author of the novels *Contents May Have Shifted* and *Sight Hound;* two collections of linked short stories, *Cowboys Are My Weakness* and *Waltzing the Cat;* and a collection of essays, *A Little More About Me*, all published by W. W. Norton. Her stories have appeared in Best American Short Stories, O. Henry Awards, Pushcart Prize, and Best American Short Stories of the Century collections. She is the director of creative writing at the University of California–Davis and teaches in the Pacific University low-residency MFA program. She lives at nine thousand feet in Colorado, near the headwaters of the Rio Grande.

LAURA JOFRE writes about parenting and family for a variety of magazines and websites. Her work has appeared in *Self* and *Westchester Family* and on Babble.com. She lives in New York with her husband, three children, a fair amount of chaos, and a decent wine rack.

ANNA KLENKE enjoys reading, tennis, and antique quilts. Her work has been published in *The New York Times, Paper Darts,* and *Off Switch* magazine, among others. She also writes regularly for www.Care2.com and her personal blog, *Elbow Patches.*

ANN LEARY is the author of the memoir *An Innocent, a Broad* (Morrow) and the novel *Outtakes from a Marriage* (Shaye Areheart). Her new novel, *The Good House* (St. Martin's), will be published in 2013. She lives with her husband and two children on a small farm in Connecticut.

LAURIE LINDEEN is the author of the memoir *Petal Pusher* (Atria), which recaps her years as a Slur Girl and beyond. She's currently working on a memoir titled *It's a Wonder We All Survived: From Free Range Wild Child to Uptight Parent.* She lives in Minnesota with her husband and son and teaches creative writing with an emphasis on memoir and essay writing.

JOYCE MAYNARD's essays and columns have appeared in numerous anthologies. Her many books include the novel *Labor Day,* soon to be released as a major motion picture, and *To Die For.* Her best-selling memoir, *At Home in the World,* has been translated into fifteen languages. Mother of three grown children, she makes her home in Northern California, where she runs seminars on the writing of memoir. Her website is www.joycemaynard.com.

DAPHNE MERKIN is a cultural critic and a contributing writer to *The New York Times Magazine, Elle,* and *Tablet.* Formerly a staff writer for *The New Yorker,* where she wrote about film, books, and figures as varied as Sigmund Freud, Marilyn Monroe, and Kurt Cobain, she continues to explore topics both high and low, including, most recently, contemporary Jewish cinema, the changing tides of child rearing, the defense of antidepressants, and designer Tory Burch.

Daphne is the author of a novel, *Enchantment*, and a collection of essays, *Dreaming of Hitler*. She lives with her daughter in New York City and is at work on a memoir, *Melancholy Baby*.

JACQUELYN MITCHARD is the author of twenty-two books of fiction for adults and children, including *The Deep End of the Ocean*, the inaugural selection of Oprah's Book Club, named by *USA Today* one of the ten most influential books of the past twenty-five years. Her second novel, *The Most Wanted*, was short-listed for the 1999 Orange Prize, and several of her young-adult books have been honored and used in school curricula across the United States. Mitchard, an adjunct professor in the MFA program in creative writing at Fairfield University, lives with her family on Cape Cod.

LIZA MONROY is the author of the novel *Mexican High*. Her essays and articles have appeared in *The New York Times*, *Newsweek*, the *Los Angeles Times*, *Self*, and other publications. She lives and writes in Brooklyn, New York, where she is currently at work on a memoir and teaches writing at Columbia University and online.

ASRA Q. NOMANI is a former *Wall Street Journal* reporter. Born in Mumbai, India, she grew up in a conservative Muslim family that banned alcohol. After 9/11, Nomani dedicated herself to challenging extremist ideas and to invoking common sense, including regarding the consumption of alcohol.

ELISSA SCHAPPELL is the author of two books of fiction, *Blueprints for Building Better Girls* and *Use Me*, which was a finalist for the PEN/Hemingway Award. She is a contributing editor at *Vanity Fair*, where she writes the "Hot Type" column, a cofounder of and editor at large at TinHouse.com, and a former senior editor of the *Paris Review*. Her short stories, essays, and nonfiction have appeared in *The Paris Review*, *BOMB*, *One Story*, *SPIN*, *Vogue*, *The New York Times*

Book Review, *Book Forum*, and other publications, and in anthologies such as *The KGB Bar Reader*, *The Bitch in the House*, *The Mrs. Dalloway Reader*, and *Cooking and Stealing*. She lives in Brooklyn.

HELENE STAPINSKI is the author of two memoirs: *Five-Finger Discount: A Crooked Family History* and *Baby Plays Around: A Love Affair, with Music*. She's written for *The New York Times*, *Travel & Leisure*, *Food & Wine*, Salon.com, *Real Simple*, and other newspapers and magazines. She's been a featured performer with the Moth's "Spoken Word" series, has taught creative writing at New York University and Fordham, and lectures regularly at Columbia University, where she was a graduate fellow in the MFA program.

LIANNE STOKES, like any white girl who got an 820 on her SATs, became a nonfiction writer. She's written for *Interview*, *Playgirl*, The Frisky.com, and the anthology *Rejected: Tales of the Failed, Dumped, and Canceled*. Her debut memoir is aptly called *Below Average: A Lifetime Way Under the Bar*. In her spare time she talks to herself. And yes, she really thinks someone is listening.

EVA TENUTO is a writer, actor, and director. She studied acting at the American Academy of Dramatic Arts and went on to found the Women's Experimental Theater Group. Based out of New York City, the WETG wrote, directed, and produced original material based on real-life experiences for over a decade. Her latest venture is the TMI Project (www.tmiproject.org), a nonprofit organization she founded that empowers teens and adults through writing and performance workshops.

EMMA KATE TSAI is a writer and editor in Houston, Texas. She graduated from the University of Houston and has a master's degree in liberal studies from Rice University. Her artistic interests lie in memoir and personal essay, and her creative writing has been published in several online publications, including the blog Feaston Love.com. Her full-length memoir on identity as an identical twin, *Say My Name,* is in draft form.

PRISCILLA WARNER coauthored the *New York Times* bestselling memoir *The Faith Club,* then toured the country for three years, popping Klonopin to ward off panic attacks. In the skies above Oklahoma, she read about Tibetan monks who meditated so effectively that neuroscientists were studying their brains. Vowing to find her inner monk, Priscilla learned how to meditate, chronicling her adventures with teachers, healers, therapists, monks, and mystics in her bestselling memoir *Learning to Breathe: My Yearlong Quest to Bring Calm to My Life.*

RITA WILLIAMS is the author of *If the Creek Don't Rise.* Her work has appeared in *Best Food Writing 2007,* the *Los Angeles Times, O, The Oprah Magazine, O At Home, Saveur,* the *Utne Reader,* and *Fins and Feathers.* She is a contributing editor to the *Los Angeles Review of Books* and teaches in the Master of Professional Writing Program at the University of Southern California. She is currently writing a novel.

ABOUT THE EDITORS

CAREN OSTEN GERSZBERG is
a freelance writer and cofounder of
Drinking Diaries.com. Caren's articles
and essays have appeared in *The New
York Times, Travel & Leisure, National
Geographic Traveler, Parents,* and other
national magazines and websites. She
wrote a NYTimes.com column, "Mom
U," about her daughter's college ad-
missions experience, and currently blogs both at HuffingtonPost
.com and on her travel blog, Embark, at www.carenosten.com.

Born and raised in New York, Caren graduated from the University of Pennsylvania and earned a dual master's degree in French
and journalism from New York University. Her career in publishing began with a summer job at French *Vogue* in Paris, which paved
the way for a full-time position at *Mademoiselle* in New York. After
four years as a research editor at *Rolling Stone,* Caren launched her
freelance career and also became the New York correspondent for
French *Glamour,* writing a monthly column in French.

Caren has taught feature writing as an adjunct professor at New
York University's Arthur L. Carter Journalism Institute. A passionate traveler, Caren lives in Westchester County, New York, with her
husband and three children.

LEAH ODZE EPSTEIN is the cofounder of Drinking Diaries.com. Born and raised in Bethesda, Maryland, Leah got her BA in English from Cornell University. She worked as a news assistant at *The New York Times*, an adjunct professor of writing at Baruch College, and an assistant editor at One World/Ballantine Books.

Leah has written freelance book and movie reviews for publications including *Publisher's Weekly* and *Bookpage* and has worked as a freelance editor and copy editor. Leah writes fiction for young adults and poetry, and blogs for HuffingtonPost.com. Leah loves to read, write, and run. She lives in Westchester County, New York, with her husband and three children.

ACKNOWLEDGMENTS

Our biggest thank-you goes to all the writers who have generously shared their stories on our blog, DrinkingDiaries.com, and to those who have written essays for this book. Without your openness and willingness to take a risk, this anthology, and the blog, would not exist.

We couldn't have started our blog, the seed for this book, without the generosity and guidance of Gretchen Rubin. Our gratitude also goes to Priscilla Warner, who helped us every step of the way—from book proposal on.

We'd like to thank our editor, Brooke Warner, and the staff at Seal Press for their support, and our agent, Jill Marsal, whose expertise was much needed and appreciated. Our gratitude to Elizabeth Kaplan—the first to realize this project's potential.

Many thanks to Jacques Steinberg and Jean Chatzky for their friendship and encouragement throughout. We are grateful to Palmer Davis, who used his special camera lens to make us look that much better. And to Damon Mastandrea, our web wizard, for rescuing us time and time again from technical emergencies. Also, a huge thank-you to Suzanne Beilenson for her marketing genius (and help with titles).

We have been fortunate to have people give us an additional forum to share our collective stories: Margaret Wheeler Johnson and Jessica Rotondi at HuffingtonPost.com, Anna David and Maer Roshan at TheFix.com, Lynda from LarchmontDish.com, Courtney Helgoe at *Experience Life* magazine, and Felice Shapiro at BA50.com.

We'd also like to thank our friends, families, and specifically our husbands, Rich and Paul, and our children—Nicole, Emily, and Simon; Edie, Lily, and Julian—for their love, support, and overall tolerance of our endless analyses and discussions of drink.

Cheers to you all!

—Caren and Leah

SELECTED TITLES FROM SEAL PRESS

For more than thirty years, Seal Press has published groundbreaking books. By women. For women.

Dancing at the Shame Prom: Sharing the Stories That Kept Us Small, edited by Amy Ferris and Hollye Dexter. $15.00, 978-1-58005-416-4. A collection of funny, sad, poignant, miraculous, life-changing, and jaw-dropping secrets for readers to gawk at, empathize with, and laugh about—in the hopes that they will be inspired to share their secret burdens as well.

Loaded: Women and Addiction, by Jill Talbot. $14.95, 978-1-58005-218-4. A poignant, gut-wrenching memoir of one woman's complicated relationship with multiple addictions.

Addicted Like Me: A Mother-Daughter Story of Substance Abuse and Recovery, by Karen Franklin and Lauren King. $16.95, 978-1-58005-286-3. A mother and daughter share their candid struggles with addiction—thirty years apart—giving readers insight into how to break the cycle.

Licking the Spoon: A Memoir of Food, Family, and Identity, by Candace Walsh. $16.00, 978-1-58005-391-4. The story of how—accompanied by pivotal recipes, cookbooks, culinary movements, and guides—one woman learned that you can not only recover but blossom after a comically horrible childhood if you just have the right recipes, a little luck, and an appetite for life's next meal.

Inappropriate Random: Stories on Sex and Love, edited by Amy Prior. $13.95, 978-1-58005-099-9. This collection of short fiction by women writers takes a hard look at love today—exposing its flaws with unflinching, often hilarious, candor.

Body Outlaws: Rewriting the Rules of Beauty and Body Image, edited by Ophira Edut, foreword by Rebecca Walker. $15.95, 978-1-58005-108-8. Filled with honesty and humor, this groundbreaking anthology offers stories by women who have chosen to ignore, subvert, or redefine the dominant beauty standard in order to feel at home in their bodies.

Find Seal Press Online
www.SealPress.com
www.Facebook.com/SealPress
Twitter: @SealPress